Layman's Bible Book Commentary
Ezra, Nehemiah, Esther, Job

LAYMAN'S BIBLE BOOK COMMENTARY

L B
B C

EZRA, NEHEMIAH, ESTHER, JOB
VOLUME 7

Mary Frances Owens

BROADMAN PRESS
Nashville, Tennessee

© Copyright 1983 • Broadman Press

All rights reserved.

4211-77

ISBN: 0-8054-1177-1

Dewey Decimal Classification: 222.7

Subject Headings: BIBLE. O. T. EZRA/ /BIBLE. O. T.
NEHEMIAH/ /BIBLE. O. T. ESTHER/ /
BIBLE. O. T. JOB

Library of Congress Catalog Number: 80-66542

Printed in the United States of America

Library of Congress Cataloging in Publication Data

Owens, Mary Frances.
  Ezra, Nehemiah, Esther, Job.

  (Layman's Bible book commentary; v. 7)
  1. Bible. O.T. Ezra—Commentaries. 2. Bible.
O.T. Nehemiah—Commentaries. 3. Bible. O.T.
Esther—Commentaries. 4. Bible. O.T. Job—
Commentaries. I. Title. II. Series.
BS1355.3.093   1984   222   80-66542
ISBN 0-8054-1177-1

Dedicated to my husband,
who has taught me to love the Old Testament

Foreword

The *Layman's Bible Book Commentary* in twenty-four volumes was planned as a practical exposition of the whole Bible for lay readers and students. It is based on the conviction that the Bible speaks to every generation of believers but needs occasional reinterpretation in the light of changing language and modern experience. Following the guidance of God's Spirit, the believer finds in it the authoritative word for faith and life.

To meet the needs of lay readers, the *Commentary* is written in a popular style, and each Bible book is clearly outlined to reveal its major emphases. Although the writers are competent scholars and reverent interpreters, they have avoided critical problems and the use of original languages except where they were essential for explaining the text. They recognize the variety of literary forms in the Bible, but they have not followed documentary trails or become preoccupied with literary concerns. Their primary purpose was to show what each Bible book meant for its time and what it says to our own generation.

The Revised Standard Version of the Bible is the basic text of the *Commentary*, but writers were free to use other translations to clarify an occasional passage or sharpen its effect. To provide as much interpretation as possible in such concise books, the Bible text was not printed along with the comment.

Of the twenty-four volumes of the *Commentary*, fourteen deal with Old Testament books and ten with those in the New Testament. The volumes range in pages from 140 to 168. Four major books in the Old Testament and five in the New are treated in one volume each. Others appear in various combinations. Although the allotted space varies, each Bible book is treated as a whole to reveal its basic message with some passages getting special attention. Whatever plan of Bible study the reader may follow, this *Commentary* will be a valuable companion.

Despite the best-seller reputation of the Bible, the average survey of Bible knowledge reveals a good deal of ignorance about it and its primary meaning. Many adult church members seem to think that its study is intended for children and preachers. But some of the newer translations have been making the Bible more readable for all ages. Bible study has branched out from Sunday into other days of the week, and into neighborhoods rather than just in churches. This *Commentary* wants to meet the growing need for insight into all that the Bible has to say about God and his world and about Christ and his fellowship.

BROADMAN PRESS

Unless marked otherwise, Scripture quotations are from the Revised Standard Version of the Bible, copyrighted 1946, 1952, © 1971, 1973.

Contents

EZRA

Introduction 15

A Return by Decree (1:1 to 6:22) 17
Cyrus, Instrument of God (1:1-4) 17
Response to Cyrus' Decree (1:5 to 2:70) 18
Religious Life Revived (3:1-11) 20
A Look Backwards (3:12-13) 21
Refusal and Revenge (4:1-24) 21
Jews Vindicated (5:1 to 6:15) 23
Joyful Worship (6:16-22) 24

Ezra's Return and Reforms (7:1 to 10:44) 25
Ezra's Return from Exile (7:1-10) 26
King's Commission to Ezra (7:11-26) 27
Ezra's Doxology (7:27-28) 28
A Great Caravan (8:1-20) 29
Prayer for Protection (8:21-23) 30
Holy Men and Holy Vessels (8:24-30) 32
Arrival at Jerusalem (8:31-36) 33
Ezra's Grief over Israel's Sin (9:1-15) 34
The People's Response (10:1-15) 36
Repentance and Reform (10:16-44) 37

NEHEMIAH

Introduction 39

The Rebuilding Program (1:1 to 6:14) 40

A Distressing Report (1:1-11)   40
Permission and Investigation (2:1-16)   42
Announcement and Opposition (2:17-20)   43
List of the Assignments (3:1-32)   45
Resolve in the Face of Opposition (4:1-23)   46
Financial Problems of Judah (5:1-19)   49
Plots Against Nehemiah (6:1-14)   51

Completion, Census, and Congregation (6:15 to 8:18)   52
The Wall Completed (6:15-19)   53
Watchmen Appointed (7:1-3)   54
The Census (7:4-73a)   54
Congregating to Hear the Law (7:73b to 8:18)   55

Confession and Dedication Ceremonies (9:1 to 12:47)   56
Repentance and Reform (9:1 to 10:39)   56
Repopulating Jerusalem (11:1 to 12:47)   59

The Reforms of Nehemiah (13:1-31)   61
Tobiah's Expulsion (13:1-9)   62
Restoring Support for the Levites (13:10-14)   62
Sabbath Reforms (13:15-22)   63
Mixed Marriage Reforms (13:23-29)   64
Summary of Reforms (13:30-31)   65

ESTHER

Introduction   66

The King's Decree (1:1-22)   67
A Royal Feast (1:1-9)   68
Queen Vashti Replaced (1:10-22)   68

Esther: The New Queen (2:1-23)   69
Parade of Beautiful Women (2:1-4)   69
Background of Mordecai and Esther (2:5-11)   70

King's Selection of Esther (2:12-23)   71

Haman's Promotion and Edict (3:1-15)   72
    Haman's Anger (3:1-11)   72
    Notifying the Officials (3:12-15)   73

Plan to Intercede (4:1 to 5:14)   73
    Esther's Distress About the Plot (4:1-9)   73
    Further Exchange of Messages (4:10-17)   74
    Esther's First Request (5:1-8)   74
    Haman's False Security (5:9-14)   75

King's Honor of Mordecai (6:1 to 7:10)   76
    Mordecai's Deed Rewarded (6:1-11)   76
    Haman's Distress (6:12-14)   76
    Esther's Petition (7:1-6)   77
    Haman's Execution (7:7-10)   78

Jews Given Their Revenge (8:1-17)   78
    Esther's Courageous Intercession (8:1-6)   79
    King's New Edict (8:7-14)   79
    Mordecai's Promotion Made Public (8:15-17)   80

Destruction and Feast (9:1-32)   80
    Jews' Destruction of Enemies (9:1-19)   80
    Origin of Feast of Purim (9:20-32)   81

Appendix of Book (10:1-3)   82

JOB

Introduction   84

Job's Background and Situation (1:1 to 2:13)   86
    Character and Status of Job (1:1-5)   87
    Job's Trials Begin (1:6-22)   88

His Trials Increase (2:1-13) 90

First Round of the Debate (3:1 to 14:22) 92
    Job: First Round (3:1-26) 93
    Eliphaz: First Round (4:1 to 5:27) 94
    Job's Response (6:1 to 7:21) 95
    Bildad: First Round (8:1-22) 97
    Job's Response (9:1 to 10:22) 97
    Zophar: First Round (11:1-20) 99
    Job's Final Response in First Round (12:1 to 14:22) 99

Second Round of the Debate (15:1 to 21:34) 102
    Eliphaz: Second Round (15:1-35) 102
    Job: Second Round (16:1 to 17:16) 103
    Bildad: Second Round (18:1-21) 105
    Job's Response (19:1-29) 106
    Zophar: Second Round (20:1-29) 108
    Job's Final Response in Second Round (21:1-34) 109

Third Round of the Debate (22:1 to 31:40) 112
    Eliphaz: Third Round (22:1-30) 112
    Job: Third Round (23:1 to 24:25) 114
    Bildad: Third Round (25:1-6) 116
    Job's Response (26:1-4) 117
    Bildad's Psalm (26:5-14) 117
    Job's Response (27:1-7) 118
    Zophar: Third Round (27:8-23) 118
    Wisdom Poem (28:1-28) 119
    Job: Final Response in Third Round (29:1 to 31:40) 120

Elihu Prepares Ground for God's Speeches (32:1 to 37:24) 125
    Elihu's Speeches Begin (32:1-22) 126
    God's Redemptive Purpose (33:1-33) 127
    Defense of God's Justice (34:1 to 35:16) 128
    Elihu's Concluding Statements (36:1 to 37:24) 130

Speeches of the Lord (38:1 to 42:6) 132
    The Lord's First Speech (38:1 to 40:2) 132
    Job's Response (40:3-5) 134

The Lord's Second Speech (40:6 to 41:34)   135
Job's Final Response (42:1-6)   136

Epilogue (42:7-17)   137
Judgment on the Friends (42:7-9)   137
Job's Fortunes Restored (42:10-17)   138

EZRA

Introduction

The events recorded in Ezra took shape against a background of national disaster. Nebuchadnezzar's army had leveled the Temple at Jerusalem and destroyed most of Judah about 587 BC. Thousands had lost their lives either as a direct or indirect result of the battles. In addition, Nebuchadnezzar had deported Judah's best leadership to Babylon. These talented leaders had the potential to become an asset to their captors.

Those Jews who remained in their homeland faced a pitiful existence. They lacked leadership, unity, a worship center, and basic possessions. Actually, the deported Jews fared better than the ones who remained at home. However, both groups experienced loneliness and bitterness. From outward appearances, Judah's defeat seemed to bring its national existence to an end. The nation had prided itself on being "God's people." From all external signs, these same people had become "no people." No wonder they became disillusioned about their status.

The spiritual "backsliding" of the Jews who remained in Judah reflects this disillusionment. They used the destruction of the Temple as an excuse for not worshiping. They made no serious effort to reestablish worship of the Lord. The Book of Jeremiah indicates that the Jews who fled to Egypt likewise failed to preserve the faith of their fathers. The exiles to Babylon, meanwhile, also went through an extreme test of faith. However, the influence of the prophets helped to keep the exiles there in touch with the Jewish religion.

The narrative of the Book of Ezra begins at the time when King Cyrus of Persia conquered Babylon. As a study of chapter 1 will reveal, Cyrus's conquest of Babylon paved the way for the events described in Ezra. The gradual return of the exiles to Judah and their beginning efforts to rebuild the Temple form the theme of this book.

In ancient times the Books of Ezra and Nehemiah circulated as one unit, rather than two. First and 2 Chronicles may have also formed part of the unit. Although Ezra appears before Nehemiah in Bible order, most biblical scholars believe that it actually follows Nehemiah from a chronological standpoint. Admittedly, the dating of the Books of Ezra and Nehemiah presents a complex problem. If the Book of Nehemiah belongs to the time of Artaxerxes I, as appears to be the case from some convincing evidence, a question still remains. Does Ezra merely belong to a later time in the reign of Artaxerxes I, or does it belong to the time of Artaxerxes II? (Ezra refers to the king only as Artaxerxes, without identifying which one.) Ezra and Nehemiah clearly have interwoven material. The "Chronicler" usually receives credit for both books. However, scribes like Ezra could have written the material.

Ezra covers a period from 538 BC until about 400 BC. Fifty or more years elapsed between the events of chapter 6 and those of chapter 7. The book contains no information as to what happened during that interval. The narrative begins with an account of King Cyrus's decree to the Jews to return to Jerusalem and rebuild the house of the Lord. It ends with an account of Ezra's demand that the returned exiles leave their foreign wives. The narrative includes a list of the men who met this demand.

Ezra falls naturally into two divisions. Chapters 1 to 6 deal with the return of Zerubbabel and Sheshbazzar to Jerusalem to dedicate the beginning of the Temple rebuilding project. Chapters 7 to 10 tell of the return of Ezra and his caravan to Jerusalem. They also discuss Ezra's reforms. The book concludes without mentioning the time or circumstances of Ezra's death.

Eight rulers served during the Ezra-Nehemiah era. The following chronological chart shows the history of that period in perspective. Although the reign of Cyrus over Persia began in 550 BC, his reign over Babylon did not begin until 539 BC.

Kings During Ezra-Nehemiah Era			
Cyrus	550-529 BC	Artaxerxes I	465-425 BC
Cambyses	529-521 BC	Xerxes II	425 BC
Darius I	521-486 BC	Darius II	425-404 BC
Xerxes I	486-465 BC	Artaxerxes II	404-358 BC

A Return by Decree
1:1 to 6:22

God revealed his greatness in various ways in the Ezra-Nehemiah era. He delivered his people from exile, provided for the rebuilding of the Temple and return of the vessels, and made possible the rebuilding of the walls of Jerusalem. However, readers sometimes overlook another revelation of his greatness—his ability to use unlikely instruments for the fulfilling of the divine purpose. The Book of Ezra begins with an account of how God chose a surprising tool to accomplish his goal. The man not only came from a non-Jewish background but also reigned as a foreign, conquering king.

The introduction to this commentary has already explained the historical setting of Ezra. The Jews had lived in Babylonian Exile for a long time prior to Persia's conquest of Babylon. (Jerusalem had fallen in 587 BC, and the conquest of Babylon by Persia occurred in 539 BC.) Chapter 1 reveals the mighty hand of God providing a way of deliverance for his people through a Gentile king, Cyrus of Persia.

Cyrus, Instrument of God (1:1-4)

The Book of Ezra begins with the repetition of the account with which 2 Chronicles ends: the decree of Cyrus. The decree narrated in verses 1-4 paved the way for the eventual return of many Jewish exiles to their homeland. The Chronicler states that Cyrus's main reason for allowing the Jewish exiles to return to Jerusalem was to rebuild God's house there. Nebuchadnezzar's military forces had destroyed the Temple and conquered Jerusalem.

The Lord stirred up the spirit of Cyrus (1:1-2).—Verses 1-2 suggest two truths: (1) the Lord can work through persons not generally considered to be God's Chosen People; and (2) Cyrus, though a Gentile, was receptive to God and gracious toward the people whom he conquered.

Verse 1 dates the decree mentioned in verse 2. The phrase "first year of Cyrus king of Persia" (1:1) means the first year that the Persian king reigned over Babylon after the conquest, about 538 BC, not the first year Cyrus ruled over Persia, 550 BC. This verse concerning Cyrus's decree brings to mind the prophecy of Jeremiah 31:38: "Behold, the days are coming . . . when the city shall be rebuilt for the Lord."

A person stirred by God does not necessarily grasp the full import of what God inspired him to say. Even the prophets could not fully perceive the messages they delivered under divine inspiration. God "stirred up" King Cyrus and used him to carry forward the divine plan of restoring God's people and rebuilding the Temple, but Cyrus could not have fully understood God's purpose in doing it.

The king's instructions (1:3-4).—King Cyrus decreed that the Jews begin returning to their homeland. (The exiles did not all return at the same time; in fact, some did not choose to return at all.) Cyrus expressed the wish that the God of the returning Jews go with them to Jerusalem to rebuild God's house. The last part of verse 3 ("he is the God who is in Jerusalem") reflects the ancient idea that each territory had its own deity.

The king instructed those of the exiles who chose to remain in Babylon to support the efforts of their returning Jewish brethren. They received orders to furnish supplies and offerings for the travelers and for the Temple (v. 4). The writer of Ezra made no reference to the irony of a Gentile king having to instruct his Jewish subjects to help each other.

From studying verses 1-4, then, we see how Cyrus, a Gentile king, became an instrument of God to restore the Jewish nation. The emphasis does not lie so much on Cyrus' tolerant attitude toward his conquered subjects as on the power of God. The Lord used a Gentile king to rebuild God's house at Jerusalem and to reestablish the Jewish community in its homeland.

Response to Cyrus' Decree (1:5 to 2:70)

Verse 5 implies that the heads of the Jewish tribes made a positive and immediate response to Cyrus's decree. The "heads of the fathers' houses" (v. 5) enthusiastically rose up with the intention of returning to Jerusalem and rebuilding the Temple. Jewish tribes were first divided into families or clans, then subdivided into houses. First and 2 Chronicles, Ezra, and Nehemiah all view the tribes of Judah and Benjamin as the true representatives of the people of God. The heads of these two tribes set the example of zeal in wanting to rebuild God's house in Jerusalem.

The priests and Levites joined the heads of the tribes in their ambitious mission. They could make a much needed contribution to the Temple project. The priests and Levites both came from the priestly order, but they evidently had some differences in actual function. Numbers 18:6 indicates that the Levites acted as servants or ministers to the priests, assuming various responsibilities in the sanctuary. The priests ("Aaron's sons") functioned at the altar. In verse 1 the writer said that the Lord stirred up the spirit of Cyrus; in verse 5 he speaks of *"every one* whose spirit God had stirred" (author's italics). The Lord's act of "stirring up" both Cyrus and the Jews shows that God took the initiative in fulfilling the divine purpose. This purpose included the deliverance of his people.

Gathering the supplies and vessels (1:6-11).—Verse 6 indicates that those Jews who did not join the returning exiles helped to supply their needs by adding freewill offerings to the supplies already given. Cyrus himself returned the Temple worship vessels that Nebuchadnezzar (Judah's former conqueror) had removed from Jerusalem and had placed in the house of his own gods. The treasurer officially counted out the vessels and gave them to Sheshbazzar, a leader ("prince") of the tribe of Judah. The number of gold and silver vessels returned to the Jews is variously reported at 5,469 (RSV) and 5,400 (KJV).

Categories of the returnees (2:1-70).—Chapter 2 contains a list of the first group of exiles who returned home from captivity. Verses 3-67 list an astounding number of returnees. Ezra 1:11 seems to indicate that Sheshbazzar went first, carrying with him the gold and silver vessels that belonged in the Temple. The narrative does not indicate how many people accompanied him. Including Sheshbazzar, the account lists twelve leaders on the first major return to Jerusalem. Apparently this number alludes to the twelve tribes. The name Zerubbabel heads the list, thus suggesting his importance.

Various theologians have attempted to divide the lists contained in verses 3-67 into categories. Biblical scholar Jacob M. Myers suggests this division: laymen identified by family (vv. 2*b*-19); identification by place (vv. 20-35); priestly families (vv. 36-39); Levites (vv. 40)· singers (v. 41); gatekeepers (v. 42); Temple slaves (vv. 43-54); Solomon's servants (vv. 55-58); those without proof of ancestry (vv. 59-63); and the total congregation (vv. 64-67). Upon arriving at Jerusalem, the heads of some of the families gave liberal offerings to be used for the rebuilding of God's house. The various returnees then began the process of settling into their own town—no small task, under the circumstances.

The response to Cyrus's decree had been great. Verse 64 totals the number of the group as 42,360 persons, plus numerous servants, singers, and an extensive collection of work animals. Nevertheless, this was only one of several large groups of returning exiles that eventually responded to Cyrus's decree. Ezra later led another of the major returns.

Religious Life Revived (3:1-11)

Ezra's account indicates that the next event took place at the beginning of the seventh month after the return of the group of exiles led by Zerubbabel. The resettled people gathered in Jerusalem. Jeshua (the first post-Exilic high priest), his fellow priests, and Zerubbabel and his kinsmen built an altar to God. Erection of the altar would enable them to offer burnt sacrifices before rebuilding the Temple. The builders constructed the altar according to the prescription contained in Exodus 20:25.

The meaning of 3:3 poses somewhat of a problem. The question relates to the connection between the setting of the altar in place and the Jews' fear of the "peoples of the lands." Verse 3 may mean that the people of Israel rebuilt the altar in defiance of the objection of hostile neighbors. However, it may relate, instead, to the rebuilding of the altar as a means of remaining in God's favor—a necessity if the Jews expected God's help in defense against foes.

The project begins (3:5-11).—The concluding comment in 3:6 sets the stage for what follows. Evidently the fact that the people of Israel had not yet rebuilt the Temple lay heavy on the consciences of the religious leaders. Verse 7 indicates that the leaders began making arrangements for the rebuilding process. The stone masons and carpenters received wages in the form of metal coins for quarrying and carving stones for the Temple. However, the same verse implies that payment of other workers took the form of commodities, rather than coins. For example, the tradesmen of Sidon and Tyre, who brought the famous cedar trees from Lebanon to use as timber for the beams, received payment in the form of food, drink, and oil. Cyrus's decree (1:2-4) contains no record of the grant mentioned in verse 7.

During the second year of the project, the Levites received appointment to oversee the work (vv. 8-9). The laying of the foundation of the Temple prompted a joyous celebration. Praise to God took the form of trumpet blowing by the priests, cymbal playing by the Levites, and responsive singing of a hymn of praise and thanksgiving based on Psalm 106:1.

The earlier erecting of an altar, and particularly the beginning of the rebuilding of the Temple, marked a reviving of the religious life of Judah. In essence, the Jews who had viewed themselves as "no people" because of their defeat and exile, now resumed the self-image of "God's people."

A Look Backwards (3:12-13)

Memories of the "good old days" can dull one's vision to the hope of the present and future. Such became the case of some of the elders of Israel who could take a mental look backwards to the original Temple in all its glory. The foundation of the new Temple would naturally seem a far cry from the former completed splendor of the old Temple. Understandably, therefore, the elders "wept with a loud voice" while the others "shouted aloud for joy" (v. 12). Whether intentionally or not, the writer inserted a note of humor in relating his account of the incident. He commented: "People could not distinguish the sound of the joyful shout from the sound of the people's weeping, for the people shouted with a great shout, and the sound was heard afar" (v. 13).

Several factors may have precipitated the weeping of the older men. Nostalgia over the beauty of the first Temple and memory of its terrible destruction probably caused the elders to mourn. They likely considered the old Temple irreplaceable. (People of today sometimes experience the same kind of nostalgia when a new church building must replace a deteriorated one.) However, the time had come for the people of Judah to stop looking back and focus on hope for the future. God made possible the rebuilding of the Temple—an accomplishment that probably had looked futile during the dark years of exile.

Refusal and Revenge (4:1-24)

News of the rebuilding project soon reached the Samaritans. The Samaritans had wanted to join with the Jews in rebuilding the

Temple. They reasoned that they worshiped the same God as the Jews, so why should not they participate in the rebuilding, and later in worship, there? However, the Jews took a dim view of the offer. They regarded Samaritans as people of mixed blood who had no business polluting Jewish worship. The Jews told the Samaritans that King Cyrus had given the order to rebuild God's house to the Jews, not the Samaritans. Actually, though, a more basic reason was the traditional enmity between Jews and Samaritans. The Jews did not want these adversaries to have any part in the undertaking.

Seeking revenge (4:4-16).—"The people of the land" (4:4), presumably the Samaritans, sought revenge by undermining the morale of the Temple builders. They employed counselors to frustrate the efforts of the Jews during the reigns of Cyrus, Cambyses, and Darius. During the reign of Xerxes I ("Ahasuerus") the Samaritans sent a letter of complaint to the king about the Jews. The writer of Ezra did not reveal the contents of this first letter, but he revealed the contents of a second letter to the next king, Artaxerxes (vv. 11-16). The Revised Standard Version states that the Samaritans wrote it in Aramaic; the King James Version, Syrian (v. 7).

In brief, the second letter accused the Jewish community of plotting against the empire. The writers referred to Jerusalem as a rebellious and wicked city that had resolved to rebuild the walls in order to avoid paying tribute to the king. The letter also said that in the past Jerusalem had shown itself to be a seditious city (v. 15). The damaging letter concluded with a warning that if the rebuilding continued, the king might lose control of the territory. The tiny area of Judah, in comparison with the immensity of the Babylonian empire, makes the warning sound laughable to readers of today. Nevertheless, Artaxerxes took the warning seriously.

Artaxerxes' reply (4:17-24).—The king wrote a letter in answer to the charge. He reported that he had checked the history of Jerusalem. He had learned that Jerusalem did indeed have a history of rebellion and sedition and had ruled over other nations. Artaxerxes therefore added a command that the Jews cease the rebuilding of Jerusalem. In protection of his own interest, he added: "Why should damage grow to the hurt of the king?" (v. 22).

The complainants then had in hand the authority they needed to force the workers to stop. They made haste to see that the Jews obeyed the king's command. Verse 24 adds the note that at the same time the rebuilding of Jerusalem ceased, the reconstruction of the Temple came to a halt. The second letter, however, had not directly lodged any complaints about the rebuilding of the Temple.

The verses discussed above (v. 1-24) present some very difficult chronological problems, especially in regard to the reigns of the kings. Nevertheless, the Chronicler did accomplish his real purpose. He recorded, for the benefit of future generations, the reason for the long delay in completing the Temple. Persecution by enemies and an edict from the king made continuance of building virtually impossible for a long period of time.

Jews Vindicated (5:1 to 6:15)

Having explained the reason for the long delay in completing the rebuilding of the Temple, the Chronicler again picked up the thread of the rebuilding account. Ezra 5:1 to 6:15 tells of an official report of the renewed construction efforts and of the subsequent vindication of the Jews.

Chapter 5 points out the influence of Haggai and Zechariah, prophets of Judah, upon the completion of the Temple rebuilding. Their prophecies stirred up the people to return to the task that they had begun so long ago. Zerubbabel, Jeshua, and the prophets led the way.

Preparing for a report (5:3-5).—Observing what had happened, Tattenai, a Babylonian official, confronted them with the question of where they had received permission to continue the building of walls and Temple. (Previously the king had told them to stop their work until he ordered differently.) Tattenai also asked the names of the workers so that he could send an accurate report to the king. The workers refused to be intimidated. God enabled them to continue the work they had begun (v. 5).

Tattenai's letter to the king (5:6-17).—As planned, Tattenai wrote a letter to King Darius and gave him a full report. He began by describing the impressive progress that the Jews had made in the building. He spoke of the stones that the workers had laid and the support beams for the roof. He told the king that he had questioned the Jews about their authority to continue the work. He also listed the builders' names.

The next part of Tattenai's letter to King Darius contained the Jews' defense of their action. The writer explained the Jewish justification in the following way. He said that the Jews claimed to be servants of God. Long ago one of their great kings (Solomon) had built a house for God. Later God had to punish the nation for its sins by allowing Nebuchadnezzar of Babylon to destroy God's house and exile his people to Babylon. When Cyrus of Persia became ruler of Babylon, however, he had ordered the rebuilding of God's house in Jerusalem. Sheshbazzar had then laid the foundation for God's house in Jerusalem, but the workers had not yet completed the Temple. (Sheshbazzar, Jehoiachin's fourth son, had been appointed by Cyrus to serve as governor.)

Having written the king about the Jewish defense for rebuilding the Temple, Tattenai requested that the king order a search in the royal archives. He wanted to know if King Cyrus had really decreed the building of the Temple. Tattenai asked King Darius to instruct him what to do about the Jewish rebuilding project.

Darius replies to Tattenai (6:1-15).—Darius investigated the Jewish claim. After he located the decree of Cyrus, Darius ordered the building of the Temple at Jerusalem as Cyrus had decreed. He prescribed the height, width, and other specifications of the Temple to conform with the earlier dimensions that he had found.

King Darius commanded that the royal treasury bear the expense and that the work be unhindered. This act made their vindication complete. The king ordered complete cooperation, threatening destruction to any person who stood in the way of the rebuilding of the Temple (6:9-12).

Tattenai immediately followed the king's orders. The Chronicler said that the command of God, plus the decree of Cyrus, Darius, and Artaxerxes, had made possible the completion of the Temple (6:15).

Joyful Worship (6:16-22)

The account of the dedication, as narrated in verses 16-22, brings to mind the celebration following the building of Solomon's Temple (1 Kings 8). In both instances the people had responded in a spirit of worship and gratitude. The Temple played a significant role in Jewish history because it symbolized God's presence with his people. The dedication of the rebuilt Temple, therefore, became an occasion for joyous celebration.

Verse 16 begins the description of the dedication ceremonies. The people who had remained in Jerusalem after the defeat, the priests and Levites, and the returned exiles all joined in the celebration. Their offerings of one hundred bulls, two hundred rams, four hundred lambs, and twelve he-goats could not compare with the number sacrificed at the dedication of Solomon's Temple. (1 Kings 8:5 states that King Solomon's congregation sacrificed so many sheep and oxen that they could not be counted.) Nevertheless, the same spirit of joyous worship characterized both events. The twelve he-goats (6:17) represented the twelve tribes of Israel.

The rebuilding of the Temple called for the installation of priests and Levites to serve in their respective positions in the Temple. Verse 18 explains that Mosaic law required it, but it does not specify the location in the law. Possibly, the instruction refers to Numbers 3:5-9.

Resumption of feast days (6:19-22).—The purification of the priests and Levites enabled the returned exiles to keep the Passover and the Feast of Unleavened Bread. All who had separated themselves from "the pollutions of the peoples" (v. 21—circumcised proselytes) could join the Jews in the Feast of the Passover.

Verse 22 summarizes the reasons to rejoice at these feasts. The Lord had graciously lifted up his downtrodden people. He had made possible the rebuilding of the Temple by turning the heart of the king toward the children of Israel. Verse 22 does not identify the name of the king. The term "king of Assyria" may have served as a geographical, rather than ethnic, identification. Assyria was a general reference to Mesopotamia.

Ezra's Return and Reforms
7:1 to 10:44

The second section of the book begins with chapter 7. A considerable amount of time elapsed between the events recorded in chapter 6 and those in chapter 7. Estimates of the time lapse vary

from fifty or sixty years to about one hundred and twenty years.
Historically, Ezra 7:1 to 10:44 belongs after Nehemiah 7. (Neh. 8
continues the narrative of Ezra 7:1 to 10:44.)

This section of the book deals not only with Ezra's return from
Babylonia but also with his religious reforms. Ezra viewed himself as
a man with a mission. From a political standpoint, he returned on
mission for the king. The king had instructed him to investigate how
well Judah had adhered to its law (7:14). Readers should note that
Ezra did not come as a novice in religious law. He came as an
authority figure to initiate reforms in Judah. A close tie existed
between the political and religious realm of that day. Ezra's mission,
although mainly religiously oriented, reflects this close political-
religious tie.

Ezra 7:1 to 10:44 illustrates the importance of dedicated, knowl-
edgeable leaders. Judah had become lax in keeping the religious
law. In spite of Ezra's legalistic approach, he awakened the conscience of his people and took steps to purify Judah.

Ezra's Return from Exile (7:1-10)

The discussion of chapter 2 noted that the first group of returning
exiles was only one of several groups who eventually returned. Ezra
led another major group of returnees from Babylonia to Judah.

Chapter 6 concluded with the dedication of the Temple. The
events of chapter 7, a record of Ezra's return, took place many years
later. Ezra 7:1 sets the time of the return as during the reign of
Artaxerxes, but does not identify which Artaxerxes. Two Persian
kings bore that name. (See chronological chart in Ezra introduction.)

Ezra's progenitors and his qualifications (7:1b-6).—These verses
provide a record of Ezra's background. He descended from the line
of Seraiah. The Chronicler may have provided this record in order to
show that Ezra came from priestly stock. Ezra became known as
both a priest and scribe but served more significantly in the position
of scribe. Verse 6 describes Ezra as "a scribe skilled in the law of
Moses." Furthermore, because Ezra stood in God's favor, he received all that he requested from Artaxerxes. Later verses reveal
that Ezra's requests related to the religious situation in Judah. This
non-Jewish king must have respected Ezra, or he would not have
acted so graciously. In addition, the king may have hoped that his

generosity would eventually pay off in the goodwill and loyalty of his Jewish subjects.

Return and goal (7:7-10).—According to verse 7, Ezra had brought with him the same classes of Jews listed in the first return. (See ch. 2.) The dating of verses 7-8 depends on whether the "king" refers to Artaxerxes I or II. Assuming that Artaxerxes II reigned then, the time would have been about 398 BC. Ezra and his group arrived in July-August ("fifth month").

Verse 9 credits the "good hand of God" with making possible Ezra's return. Ezra returned with the intention of studying the law, putting it into practice, and teaching it well (7:10).

King's Commission to Ezra (7:11-26)

Having revealed Ezra's purpose in returning, the Chronicler reported the favorable nature of Ezra's send-off. Verses 11-26 contain a record of Artaxerxes' commission to Ezra in the form of a letter.

Three facts brought to light by the letter make the letter especially impressive: (1) the Persian king's high regard for Ezra, (2) the extreme generosity of the king, and (3) the king's knowledge of Jewish affairs. Evidently Ezra held a high position in the Persian government, probably as a court officer in charge of Jewish affairs. His position as a Jewish official in the Persian government enabled him to serve his own people and the Lord in a unique way.

Verse 11 introduces the letter that follows. It explains that King Artaxerxes gave the letter to Ezra, the priest-scribe, who knew the commandments and statutes of the God of Israel. The letter itself started with an identification of the writer, Artaxerxes, who bore the title "king of kings" (7:12). The king addressed the document to Ezra, "priest, the scribe of the law of the God of heaven" (an official title).

The body of the letter begins in verse 13 with a decree that any of the exiled people or their priests or Levites could feel free to return to Jerusalem with Ezra. Ezra's mission was to examine the religious life of Judah and to transport the king's gifts to the God of Israel. The king further instructed Ezra to collect money from non-Jews under Artaxerxes' rule, as well as the freewill offerings of the Jews and their priests.

Conditions of the offer (7:17-23).—The king laid down specific terms of the decree. He expected Ezra to use the money exactly for its intended purpose. Ezra must use the money to buy animals for the meat offerings and cereal and drink offerings. (Cereal offerings are mentioned in RSV but not in KJV.) Within the framework of the king's terms and the will of God, Ezra had the authority to use the remaining silver and gold according to his own discretion. The king ordered Ezra to bring the Temple vessels to the Temple. These "vessels" could have been either the ones plundered by King Nebuchadnezzar or new ones.

Artaxerxes made the generous offer that if Ezra needed more money for the Temple, he could get it from the king's treasury. The king had treasury houses at various locations in the Persian empire. Ezra also had the authority to request funds at these other locations. Artaxerxes addressed these treasurers directly, commanding them to fulfill Ezra's requests diligently. Ezra was not to view the king's offer as a blank check, however. Artaxerxes set the following limits on the amount that Ezra could request: 100 talents of silver (more than 3¾ tons), 100 measures of wheat (650 bushels), 100 baths of wine and oil (607 gallons of each), and unlimited salt. The priests used salt for sacrifices.

Verse 23 suggests the king's motives for this great generosity. He did not want the wrath of the God of Israel to fall upon him. Besides, Judah's help might come in handy later in military battles. The king's generosity might win Judah's favor.

Ezra given authority (7:24-26).—The regional treasurers received further instructions not to tax any of the Jewish officials (v. 24). Meanwhile the king authorized Ezra to appoint magistrates and judges to administer the Jewish law. The law of God became the law of the king. Those Jews who did not obey the religious law would be liable for punishment just as much as if they had disobeyed Persian law. The king empowered Ezra to kill, banish, or imprison any offenders or confiscate their goods.

Ezra's Doxology (7:27-28)

Up to this point in the book the Chronicler had given a third-person account of the events. Verses 27-28 begin a first-person account that continues throughout the rest of the book. Ezra was the speaker.

A strange turn of events had shaped the history of Judah. Ezra, an exiled Jew, had been appointed to an official position in Babylon.

His prestige and favor in the king's sight enabled him to help his own nation in an unexpected way. Financially, the people of Judah, both those who had remained there after the defeat and also the returned exiles, had severe problems. Spiritually, they also needed a strong leader and religious reforms that would purify them. These financial and spiritual needs, plus the persecution faced by the people, had caused them to slow down the rebuilding of the Temple to a snail's pace. Ezra emerged at the right time and with the right resources to help in meeting these needs.

On the surface Ezra may have appeared to be merely an instrument of the king used for good public relations and/or political and military concerns. He saw the events in his life in a different perspective, however. Ezra viewed his role as that of a leader who could carry out God's plan for Judah. Ezra's words in verses 27-28, therefore, became a fitting doxology to honor God for what he had done.

First cause for praise (7:27).—The doxology began with praise to God for making a foreign king want to beautify the Temple of Israel's God. Ezra took no personal credit for this accomplishment; he credited God with it. Nevertheless, Ezra had succeeded in rising to the status of an official in the Persian government and had used his influence in leading the king to beautify God's house. Considering that Ezra was a Jewish subject, this was no small feat for him to achieve.

Second cause for praise (7:28).—Next, Ezra praised God for showing mercy to him in the presence of the king and his counselors. God had inspired the king to look favorably on him. Ezra took courage in the knowledge that the hand of the Lord was upon him in this undertaking. He added the further note that he personally selected the leaders who would accompany him to Jerusalem. This fact also gave Ezra reason to praise God. The king and his counselors could have insisted on making the choice themselves and forcing Ezra to abide by it. Instead, they left the choice to Ezra, enabling him to select the best available leaders to go with him.

A Great Caravan (8:1-20)

In chapter 8 Ezra listed those whom he chose to accompany him on his caravan to Jerusalem. Unlike the list of caravan members mentioned in the first major return (2:1-70), this list began with priests of the Aaronic line. The list then identified the members of twelve families of laymen who accompanied Ezra (vv. 3-14). Ezra used the ancestral names to identify the "sons" and included the number of men who came from each family.

The returnees (8:1-14).—The headcount of males who joined the group came to about 1,500, plus 38 Levites and 220 Temple slaves. In addition, wives and children probably joined the group, so the caravan included a large number of people. As mentioned in the study of the second chapter, over 42,360 had come with the first major return. Lesser returning groups had also arrived.

Ezra secured the Levites (8:15-20).—Ezra described his assembling of the caravan by the stream ("river") near the town of Ahava. For three days the group encamped there. In checking on the laymen and priests, Ezra discovered that no Levites had come with the caravan. Interpreters have speculated various reasons why the Levites had not come with the group. The Levites may have simply felt secure and comfortable in Babylonia and thought they might do better to remain there than to return to the uncertain conditions in Judah. Babylonia had been their home during the long exile.

Ezra knew that his nation would need Levites for ministries in the Temple. Therefore, he organized a plan to recruit them. He appointed nine leaders and two "men of insight" (v. 16, probably teachers) to confer with Iddo, a leader at Casiphia. The men went in order to persuade Iddo to send ministers for the Temple. By the good hand of God the committee secured the needed Levites. Thirty-eight Levites, plus 220 Temple servants who would attend the Levites, agreed to join the caravan (vv. 19-20).

Prayer for Protection (8:21-23)

Although Ezra seldom receives credit for being a great spiritual leader, he took his leadership responsibilities seriously. Chapters 7-8 have already illustrated how he used his favor in the king's sight as a means by which he could serve God and his fellow Jews. Ezra 7:28 further confirms his recognition that his personal success resulted from God's power, not his own. The wisdom Ezra showed in his choice of leaders to accompany him and his plan to secure the needed Levites give further proof of his leadership ability.

Ezra 8:21-23 again shows the seriousness with which Ezra took his leadership role. He had already made all the necessary physical preparations for the long journey to Jerusalem. The caravan would soon depart. He had one more need to resolve before leaving, however. He took the initiative for spiritual preparation by assembling the group for fasting and prayer before departure.

Fasting, a preventive measure (8:21).—The King James Version says in 8:21, "I proclaimed a fast . . . that we might afflict ourselves before our God." The Revised Standard Version changes "afflict" to "humble." The word *fast* relates to abstinence from food for a religious reason, such as repentance, calamity, mourning, and supplication. Some Old Testament passages provide insights as to the reasons for fasting. For example, relating to atonement, Leviticus 23:26 states: "You shall afflict yourself and present an offering." Another passage, 2 Samuel 12:16, tells of David's fast—a fast that resulted in punishment being transferred from himself to someone else. Still another passage, Jeremiah 36:9, speaks of Josiah proclaiming a fast for the purpose of turning away God's wrath from the people because of their sin. In these and other passages the people fasted in order to win God's favor. Presumably they believed that by afflicting themselves with hunger, they would arouse God's pity. Fasting symbolized humility, but later it became a cloak to cover unrighteousness (Isa. 58:3).

Generally, *feasting days* celebrated victory, whereas *fasting days* depicted failure (either military or moral). In Ezra's case, however, fasting had a preventive, rather than a curative motive. Ezra and his caravan wanted to begin their journey with an assurance of divine favor. Fasting illustrated to God their humility. It also prepared the way for their prayer of petition.

A realistic petition (8:22-23).—Verse 22 candidly points to a practical motive for seeking assurance of God's favor on the journey. Ezra had testified to the king in glowing terms about the power of the God of Israel. If Ezra had requested an armed escort to protect the caravan, he would have appeared not to trust God. Besides, Ezra had told the king that the "hand of our God is for good upon all that seek him, and the power of his wrath is against all that forsake him" (v. 22). If anything happened to the caravan, the king would assume that Ezra had forsaken God.

Ezra was not an idealistic young dreamer with his head in the clouds. He recognized the dangers of attack by bands of thieves, especially in the isolated desert wastes. The fact that the caravan planned to carry back valuable treasures for the Temple intensified the problem. Ezra had the responsibility of leading this large group of people safely to Jerusalem. He felt a special concern for the young children in the caravan (v. 21).

Therefore, Ezra paused for a time of fasting and prayer before departing. Verse 23 states that God listened to the petition. The eventual success of the journey shows that God not only heard but granted Ezra's request.

Holy Men and Holy Vessels (8:24-30)

Having prayed for divine protection for the journey, Ezra distributed the valuable gifts to be carried to the Temple in Jerusalem. As already indicated, Ezra recognized the danger of attack and robbery on the way. Therefore, although he trusted God to protect him, he took personal responsibility for the safe transport of the treasures sent by King Artaxerxes. He set apart holy men to carry the holy vessels to Jerusalem.

Priests and Levites assigned duties (8:24-25).—According to Numbers 3:8,31, and 4:7-15, only priests and Levites could carry sacred vessels. This law stemmed from the fact that both priests and sacred vessels had been consecrated in a special way to the Lord. Ezra honored the law by not allowing laymen to carry the treasures. Only the priests and Levites could perform this duty.

In addition to the legal regulation, another reason for the assignment was that priests and Levites would have a sobering effect on would-be thieves. Even thieves would hesitate to steal holy vessels from holy men, since both would be under divine protection. The fear that God might turn his wrath on the offender would serve as a barrier to thievery. A modern-day comparison might be the taboo of stealing a Bible.

Ezra weighed out the treasures that the priests and Levites would carry. Verse 25 lists the gifts according to their scale of value, beginning with the least valuable or more common and concluding with the highest in value. "The silver and the gold" (v. 25) refers to the freewill offerings made by the king, counselors, and noblemen, plus those collected from Jews who resided in Babylonia. Ezra designated the "vessels" as the most valuable treasure.

Guards of the treasures (8:26-30).—Verses 26-27 enumerate the amounts of the various gifts that the priests and Levites would carry. The list includes 650 talents of silver (21 tons), 100 talents of gold (over three tons), 20 golden bowls, and two copper vessels worth as much as gold. Gold carried more value than silver in that day, but fine copper equaled or surpassed gold in worth.

After distributing the treasures, Ezra reminded the priests and Levites of their own holiness (consecration) and of the holiness of the gifts they bore. Presumably, the priests served as overseers while the Levites actually carried the gifts. Both had a duty to guard and keep these gifts until their safe delivery to Jerusalem. Ezra did not infer that the "holy men" might pilfer the treasures. Rather, he affirmed the divine protection they would receive because of their religious office.

Arrival at Jerusalem (8:31-36)

Both the fasting and the distribution of the treasures to be carried took place before the caravan left Ahava. The group finally departed in April ("first month"). God protected them from enemies and ambushes along the way, as they had petitioned for him to do. (See vv. 21-23.) Ezra 7:9 had announced their arrival in Jerusalem in the fifth month. The journey, therefore, took four months. After arriving, they encamped in Jerusalem for three days before taking their gifts to the Temple. The three-day delay in going to the Temple could either have been related to a sabbath regulation or for rest and settling purposes.

Delivering the treasure (8:33-36).—On the fourth day after their arrival the responsible men brought the gifts to the Temple. Verses 25-27 have already shown the methodical inventory taken of the gifts before departure. Verses 33-34 indicate the same careful scrutiny in accounting after arrival. Evidently the checklists were compared against each other. Ezra indicates that they recorded the treasures by number and weight (v. 34). Meremoth (a priest) and other priests and Levites received the gifts from the returning exiles.

Following the presentation, the returning priests offered sacrifices at the altar. They brought burnt offerings to God, including twelve bulls, ninety-six rams, and seventy-seven lambs. They brought twelve he-goats as a sin offering.

Verse 36 informs readers that the returnees delivered the king's orders to his vice regents ("satraps") and governors. As a result, these officials had no choice but to aid the Jews and assist in whatever way they could. They "aided the people and the house of God" (v. 36).

Ezra's Grief Over Israel's Sin (9:1-15)

Some Old Testament scholars believe that the Chronicler left a gap between Ezra 8:36 and 9:1. Historian Josephus sets the events of chapter 9 as about five months after the presentation of the Temple treasures and the sacrificial offering. The problem relates to the length of time indicated by the words "after these things had been done" (v. 1).

The narrative of this chapter deals with the problem of mixed marriages in Judah and with Ezra's shock and grief concerning it. The district officials had informed Ezra that both the people and their religious leaders had married non-Jews, intermingling a holy race with heathen (foreign) neighbors. Worst of all, the chief trespassers had been the officials and leaders who should have set a good example but did not.

Intense sorrow and mourning (9:3-4).—Ezra reacted to the disconcerting news in a violent way. The tearing of his garments and pulling out of his hair symbolized sorrow and mourning, of course, but they also show concretely how strongly Ezra felt about the issue of mixed marriages. Religious law strictly prohibited marriage between the people of Israel and foreigners (Deut. 7:3). This law had a sound basis. Intermarriage with foreigners who did not worship Yahweh (the Lord) could lead to pollution of true worship by incorporating pagan practices into Jewish worship. Compromise and idolatry loomed as the possible outcome of mixed marriages. Ezra's grief about the breach caused by sin was as great as that felt by bereaved family members when a loved one died.

Ezra held a unique position in coping with the problem of mixed marriages. On one hand, he identified with his people in the sin they had committed, as verse 6 indicates. On the other hand, he identified with the righteous indignation of any faithful servant of God under these circumstances. He acted as a conscience for his people and an intercessor in their behalf at the same time. (Verses 5-15 illustrate this stance in more detail.)

When the Jews observed Ezra's intense reaction, they were terrified. Both Ezra's violently symbolic acts of self-abasement and their own awakening recognition of their sin caused them to tremble (v. 4). Meanwhile Ezra remained horror-struck ("appalled") until time for the evening sacrifices.

Ezra's prayer (9:5-9).—Verse 5 provides the first formal notice that Ezra had fasted in addition to mourning. Ezra had fasted at Ahava as a "preventive" measure to assure God's favor on the journey (8:23). He fasted in Jerusalem (v. 5) as a "curative" measure (a more common reason for fasting). However, he did it both times in preparation for prayer.

Ezra began his prayer in a spirit of humility and penitence. Even though he personally had not participated in the sin, he felt a sense of responsibility for and identity with the transgressors. He blushed (v. 6) at what his fellow Jews had done. He confessed, "Our iniquities have risen higher than our heads"—a reference to the overwhelming nature of their sin. The memory of the past sins of his nation that had been punished by defeat and exile still flooded Ezra's mind. Actually, Judah remained "to this day" (v. 7) under Persian rule. For a brief time God appeared to be in the process of restoring his remnant. The term "secure hold" in verse 8 in reference to the restoration literally means "a tent peg" (that which holds the tent in place). Ezra had rejoiced at the prospects of permanency in Judah. The settlement had revived his nation's spirit ("brighten our eyes," v. 8). God had graciously extended his steadfast love toward his people. Ezra pointed to God's provision for the rebuilding of the Temple, restoration of the ruined city, and rebuilding of the city walls.

Confession of guilt (9:10-15).—In spite of God's merciful acts, the people had forsaken God's commandments again. Ezra could only confess in shame, "And now, O our God, what shall we say after this?" (v. 10). To Ezra's credit, he did not try to hide his nation's sin or plead ignorance of God's laws. In verses 11-12 he orally reviewed the gist of many scriptural laws, rather than one specific law, as he spoke of the warning against mixed marriages.

Verses 13-15 illustrate Ezra's recognition that he and his nation did not deserve mercy. He had no right to expect forgiveness. All that Ezra could do was to confess his nation's guilt openly before God. He could only say, "Behold, we are before thee in our guilt, for none can stand before thee because of this" (v. 15).

The People's Response (10:1-15)

The Chronicler wrote in the first person form from Ezra 7:27 to
9:15. Ezra 10:1 returns to the third person form and continues in that
style for the rest of the book.

Evidently Ezra's demonstration of grief and his penitential prayer
had a great impact on the people. Although Ezra directed his prayer
to God, he also got across a message to the nation through his prayer.
Verses 1-4 describe the people's response to Ezra's dramatic actions
and prayer.

Confession and repentance (10:1-4).—The first step toward restoration must be an awareness of guilt. Confession and repentance
must follow this step. The last step involves taking concrete steps to
turn away from the sin. The people of Judah had to take all three
steps to ensure receipt of God's forgiveness.

Unlike Ezra, who merely identified with his nation in its sin, the
leaders had actually taken foreign wives for themselves. Ezra
doubtless viewed the action of the leaders as the most unconscionable of all. (An earlier passage, 9:1-3, stated that the faithlessness of
the officials and chief men had been foremost.) Shecaniah, the son of
one of the leaders, took the initiative in resolving the problem. No
evidence points to his personal guilt, but he, like Ezra, identified
with the sin of his nation and possibly even of his own father.
However, unlike Ezra, Shecaniah still saw hope in the situation
(v. 2).

Verse 3 identified the source of hope. Shecaniah proposed a
renewal of Israel's covenant with God that would involve the
discarding of foreign wives and the children of the union. Shecaniah
hoped that this reform would convince God of the sincerity of his
people's repentance. His words "according to the law" did not refer
to a law that commands an Israelite man married to a foreign wife to
divorce her. Rather, it referred to the law that Israelite men should
not marry foreign wives in the first place. The reason was that
intermarriage with heathen wives could potentially result in the
introduction of idol worship into the nation. That would defy the
most important concept of Judaism—the exclusive worship of
Yahweh as the only true God.

Readers today cringe at the thought of the tremendous suffering
involved in suddenly casting off dependent wives and children.

Apparently the logic was that a radical sin demanded a radical reform. Shecaniah interpreted Ezra's words and actions as a signal to carry out this reform. Since Ezra represented the religious law in this and other matters, he fell heir to the task of enforcing the reform. Shecaniah told Ezra that he must be strong and do it (v. 4).

Ezra's assumption of duty (10:5-11).—In order to carry out his difficult reform, Ezra needed the support of both the leaders and laymen of the nation. He therefore required them to take an oath that they would cooperate. They swore they would do it. Ezra then left the Temple to spend the night with Jehohanan where he continued to fast and mourn. (Some theologians believe that Eliashib—v. 6, the father of Jehohanan—was the high priest mentioned in Nehemiah 3:1. If so, this fact would prove that Ezra came after Nehemiah.)

The proclamation that circulated throughout Judah instructed all the returned exiles to gather at Jerusalem. The penalty for not appearing within three days would be a forfeiture of all their property and excommunication from the Jewish assembly (v. 8).

The people assembled within three days as instructed. They came in December (the ninth month by the Hebrew calendar), the season of heavy rain, and assembled outside the Temple. They had no protection from the elements. Ezra arose and told them that they must confess to God their sin of intermarriage, then separate themselves from their foreign wives (v. 11). Ezra interpreted these steps as obedience to God's will.

A practical amendment (10:12-15).—In principle the congregation agreed with what Ezra said. However, because of the large number of persons involved and the inclemency of the weather, they pled for a practical amendment to Ezra's proposal. At appointed times those who had married foreign wives would come to Jerusalem for hearings by the officials. Local elders and judges would accompany them, presumably as witnesses. In order to ensure that God's wrath had been assuaged, the hearings would not conclude until every offender had appeared. Only a small minority opposed the plan (v. 15).

Repentance and Reform (10:16-44)

The plan went as scheduled. Ezra designated by names the heads of clans to investigate each case. The hearings took three months (from the first day of the tenth month to the first day of the first month—vv. 16-17). The leaders then gave their report of the names of the offenders. Those listed pledged to put away their foreign wives.

The list began with the names of priests' families who had married foreign wives. Verses 18 and 20-22 must surely be only a partial list of the priestly families involved, since Ezra 9:1-2 implies a much larger number of guilty priests. Because of their spiritual responsibility, transgressing priests had to pay greater penalties than laymen. In addition to casting off their foreign wives and children, they had to offer a ram as a guilt offering. This requirement accords with Leviticus 5:15.

Second in the list were the Levites (v. 23). The names of the singers appeared next. The laymen, who constituted the largest group of the transgressors, were listed in verses 25-43. Whether complete or not, the list of religious leaders and laymen indicates the widespread nature of the problem.

Verse 44 states that "All these had married foreign women, and they put them away with their children." Ezra had succeeded in bringing his people to repentance and reform. He and other leaders like him in his nation's history had a purifying effect on the religious life of his people. In that respect Ezra became a positive force for righteousness in his own day.

In spite of its legalistic flavor, the Book of Ezra has some thought-provoking messages for persons of today. A brief review of the book suggests these applications. (1) God can take a devastated people and restore them through his grace and power. (2) God can use persons of all kinds and from all backgrounds to fulfill his purpose. (3) God can raise up leaders who will effectively undertake the work that needs to be done.

Ezra was only one of many leaders God raised up for a tremendous task. God has raised up leaders in our generation to keep alive true worship and to carry on his work on earth. The need for leaders to call for repentance and reform still exists today. God will prepare men and women to meet that challenge.

NEHEMIAH

Introduction

The Ezra commentary section explains the close relationship between the Books of Ezra and Nehemiah. For a review of the historic situation of the Ezra-Nehemiah era and a chronological chart of the kings, read the Ezra introduction.

The exact dating of the events of Nehemiah remains uncertain. The presumed date is between 445 and 432 BC—the twentieth to the thirty-second year of Artaxerxes' reign. Again, however, the reader must ask: Which Artaxerxes, I or II? (Actually, three kings of Persia bore this name: Longimanus, Mnemon, and Ochus.) Most scholars agree on Artaxerxes I.

Much of the Book of Nehemiah appears in autobiographical form. When the Chronicler (unknown historian) found Nehemiah's records in the Temple archives, he compiled most of the material in its original form. However, interpreters believe that the Chronicler inserted 7:72 to 9:5 from Ezra's account. Nehemiah 9:5b-37 (a penitential psalm) came from an unknown source. It may have been a commonly-used psalm for fasting days.

Nehemiah had held an honorable position ("cupbearer") in the Persian government during the Exile. Nehemiah's status in the king's sight is evident in the king's granting of the favor requested by Nehemiah. Like Ezra, Nehemiah used his prestigious position as a tool with which he could help restore the nation of Judah. In fact, the traits that best characterize Nehemiah include his nationalistic concern (ch. 1), his strong sense of religious mission (ch. 2), his authority (ch. 5), and his administrative ability (chs. 6-7).

Ezra and Nehemiah had some notable similarities. For example, both men held official positions in the Persian government, yet retained their nationalistic ties with Judah. Both had strong religious motivations. Because of Ezra's position as scribe-priest, he received credit for greater religious leadership, but Nehemiah also demonstrated religious concern and personal devotion. The main difference lay in the realm in which each man exercised his concern. Ezra's primary concerns focused on support of the Temple and on reforms that would purify the religion of his people. Nehemiah, on the other hand, dedicated himself primarily to building walls to safeguard the land that God had provided for the Jews. However, Nehemiah also served two terms as governor in Judah and actively supported social justice. In addition, he instituted various religious reforms, including taking a much more violent stand against mixed marriages than Ezra did. (See 13:23-27.)

The Rebuilding Program
1:1 to 6:14

The memoirs of Nehemiah might be called a book about a wall: a wall in ruins, a wall to rebuild, a wall to guard, a wall of opposition, and a wall to dedicate. The Babylonian destruction of Jerusalem had included the destruction of the city wall. A city wall served both a physical and psychological function in Nehemiah's day. It literally became a means of protection from enemy attack and figuratively symbolized status. Destruction of a city wall brought both vulnerability and shame upon the city's residents. The reader should not find it surprising, therefore, that the Book of Nehemiah lays so much stress on a ruined wall.

Nehemiah's account reveals more than a story about walls, however. It illustrates what can happen when capable leaders dedicate themselves to a challenging task and their people have "a mind to work" (4:6). Nehemiah's concern for his nation's welfare and his religious commitment become apparent in the reading of his account. Nevertheless, another factor becomes equally apparent. God's intervening hand in history played a strategic part in the success of Nehemiah and his fellow Jews in their momentous task.

A Distressing Report (1:1-11)

The book begins by identifying the writer of the original account and the circumstances of the events. Either Nehemiah himself, or the Chronicler who compiled the book, identified the material as an account written by Nehemiah, son of Hacaliah. The incident that precipitated the account took place during the twentieth year of the reign of Artaxerxes (Nov.-Dec., 444 BC). Nehemiah had gone to Susa, the winter residence of Persian kings.

Hanani and some other men from Judah had arrived there. They had probably come as a delegation to ask for Nehemiah's assistance in restoring Jerusalem. In the course of conversation Nehemiah learned that the survivors who had escaped exile were in great trouble (v. 3). The city wall and gates, destroyed earlier by their attackers, still lay in ruins. The plight left Jerusalem accessible to future attackers and made the city a source of derision in the eyes of hostile neighbor nations (vv. 1-3).

Verse 4 provides insight into the character of Nehemiah. Although his position of esteem in the Persian government kept him far removed from Judah's humiliation, Nehemiah wept for his fellow Jews. As indicated in the introduction, he had a great nationalistic concern. He mourned and fasted "for days" (an extended period) to show his self-abasement. (See comment on mourning and fasting, Ezra 8:21-23.) In this attitude of humility, Nehemiah prayed the prayer of supplication recorded in the next few verses.

Prayer of Nehemiah (1:5-11).—Nehemiah began his prayer with words of praise to God, not unlike the beginning of the Model Prayer given by Jesus much later. Nehemiah addressed God as the "Lord God of heaven" (same form of address for God used by King Cyrus in Ezra 1:2). The descriptive word *terrible,* used in reference to God, means awe-inspiring, not in the bad sense as the word is used today. This great and awe-inspiring God "keeps covenant and steadfast love" (v. 5, a covenant term that expresses God's enduring love for those who remain faithful and obedient to him).

Having addressed God in words of praise, Nehemiah prepared the way for the petition that he planned to make. He asked that God *hear* and *see*—listen to his petition and look at the Jews' plight with his eyes (v. 6). Nehemiah openly confessed to God the sinfulness of his people and spoke of the punishment they deserved and received. However, in verses 8-9 he also reminded God of the divine promise of restoration following his people's repentance. Verses 10-11 show how Nehemiah laid claim on that promise during the prayer. In essence he prayed that God would enable him to receive a favorable response when he approached the king with a request. The request, of course, related to permission to investigate firsthand the situation in Jerusalem.

Nehemiah would not have dared to make his request of King Artaxerxes if he had not had a position of honor in the Persian government. Verse 11 explains that Nehemiah served as the "king's cupbearer" (KJV). A cupbearer did far more than serve wine or act as a butler. The king trusted him and confided in him. The very fact that the Persian king chose a Jewish subject like Nehemiah to serve in this way is surprising. It illustrates not only Nehemiah's shrewdness, but also God's hand in the history of his people. Nehemiah's official position in Persian government became an instrument by which Judah could gain restoration. God used Nehemiah as a tool for his purpose.

Permission and Investigation (2:1-16)

Evidently Nehemiah did not immediately go to the king to make his request. According to 1:1, the delegation had come to Nehemiah in December ("Chislev"). However, Nehemiah 2:1 reveals that Nehemiah did not approach the king about the matter until April ("Nisan"). The Chronicler did not explain the reason for the delay. Nehemiah could have waited for an opportune time, or he might have felt the need of time for preparation before making the request.

Verses 1-16 deal first with Nehemiah's receipt of permission, then with his initial inspection of the city wall of Jerusalem.

The request (2:1-8).—Prior to the time mentioned in verse 1, Nehemiah had concealed his depression while in the presence of the king. During that time he had likely fasted and mourned frequently. Gradually his face had begun to show the effects of it. The king eventually noticed Nehemiah's changed appearance and diagnosed it correctly as mental, rather than physical pain. ("Heart" and "mind" have a close relationship in Jewish thought.)

Nehemiah experienced fear because of the king's observation (v. 2). However, he immediately came to the core of the matter. He reminded the king that the burial place of his ancestors (Jerusalem) lay in ruins and the city gates still remained in their burned-down condition. Nehemiah's reference to the sepulchers of his forefathers probably struck a responsive note with the king. Ancient people of all nations had respect for the burial places of their ancestors. The king asked what Nehemiah wanted to do about it, thus opening the door for the request.

Verses 5-8 deal with the particulars of Nehemiah's request. He wanted to go to Judah for the purpose of rebuilding "the city of my fathers' sepulchres." He told the king approximately how long he expected to be gone and requested official letters to the governors. He also asked for a permit for building materials with which to construct the city gates and to build himself a residence. The king granted Nehemiah permission for all that he requested.

Secret examination (2:9-16).—Nehemiah proceeded on his journey to Jerusalem. Unlike Ezra, Nehemiah had a military escort for his journey. When he arrived at the province that lay west of the Euphrates ("Beyond the River," v. 9), he gave the governors the king's letters. The three governors mentioned in verses 10 and 19 objected to Nehemiah's coming. Sanballat the Horonite (worshiper of the god, Horon) probably came from Samaria. Samaritans and Jews hated each other. Tobiah the Ammonite governed the Transjordan province of Ammon. He later plotted against Nehemiah. Geshem, the Arab governor mentioned in verse 19, shared the contempt of Sanballat and Tobiah. All these governors strongly opposed any restoration of Judah. However, because of Nehemiah's official letters and his military escort, the governors' hands were tied.

Nehemiah decided to inspect the walls secretly at night before discussing the matter with the other Jews. Only a few unmounted servants joined him for the inspection. According to verses 13-14, he went by the Valley Gate (a fortification at the northwestern corner of the City of David), then to the Dung Gate, 500 yards to the south. From there he went to the Fountain Gate, 150 yards north of the Dung Gate in the eastern part of Jerusalem, and on to the King's Pool (unknown site). He concluded the inspection by riding along the Kidron valley by the brook.

Announcement and Opposition (2:17-20)

Nehemiah 1:4 illustrated one of the characteristics of Nehemiah mentioned in the Nehemiah introduction—his nationalistic concern. Verse 20 exemplifies another one, his strong sense of religious mission. He viewed the disrepair of the city wall as a dishonor both to the nation and to God. Jerusalem had served as the religious center of Judah. To let its wall stay in disrepair amounted to an announcement to other nations that neither God nor his people had self-respect and power. From a positive standpoint, Nehemiah regarded the rebuilding of the city walls as a religious mission. Nevertheless, he could not have overlooked the political and military advantage of this move. The purpose for rebuilding the wall illustrates the close intertwining of religion and politics in ancient Judah.

Nehemiah's plan revealed (2:17-18).—Nehemiah's second tour of the city wall and gates had given him an opportunity to evaluate the extent of repair needed. By doing it at night he had avoided interference by hostile officials. Nehemiah could not keep his plan secret much longer, however. He therefore called together those classes of people mentioned in verse 16: the Jews, priests, nobles, local officials, and other builders.

Nehemiah began by confronting his listeners with the disgraceful condition of the city wall and gates. He summoned them to join him in rebuilding the wall so that they would no longer have to suffer shame. He reassured them of success with two guarantees. (1) God would guide their efforts. He had already shown favor upon Nehemiah. (2) The king had given his permission and backing for the project. These two assurances gave the people the impetus they needed. They responded by saying, "Let us rise up and build" (v. 18).

Official opposition (2:19-20).—Sanballat and Tobiah, the officials mentioned in verse 10, had reacted with hostility when Nehemiah first approached them with his letters of authority. After they heard his plan and could see his popular support, they became even more angry. They, along with Geshem the Arab, inferred that Nehemiah plotted rebellion against the king of Persia. In reality, however, their concern did not rest on the welfare of the king; they feared for their own loss of power. Until then, they had successfully kept Judah helpless under their official heels, but Nehemiah's authority and leadership posed a threat.

Nehemiah did not succumb to the intimidation of Sanballat, Tobiah, and Geshem. He responded confidently that he and his fellow Jews were on mission for God and that God would not let them fail. As for those opposing neighbors, they would have neither rights nor credits in the great work that the Jews would accomplish.

List of the Assignments (3:1-32)

Nehemiah had evidently thought through his course of action carefully. Chapters 3 and 4 imply a thorough briefing of the responsibility of each worker and his kinsmen, first in building, then in guarding the edifice. The good planning did not remove obstacles, but it did provide defense when the obstacles came.

North wall assignments (3:1-5).—Appropriately, Eliashib the high priest and the other priests rebuilt the Sheep Gate in the Temple area. They worked as far as the Hananel Tower in the northwest corner of the Temple area. The next workers on the north wall included the men of Jericho and Zaccur. The sons of Hassenaah built the Fish Gate, located in the Tyropoeon Valley and used as a port of entry for fish being carried from the seacoast. Others who worked on the north side included Meremoth, Meshullam, Zadok, and the Tekoites (natives of Tekoa, eleven miles south of Jerusalem). The *nobles* of Tekoa refused to do manual labor, however (v. 5).

West wall assignments (3:6-12).—The rebuilding of the west wall began with the Old Gate (believed to be near the Mishneh Wall). Joiada and Meshullam made that repair. The next portions of the wall were made by Melatiah who lived in Gibeon, six miles northwest of Jerusalem, and by Jadon of Meronoth (location uncertain). Uzziel, a goldsmith, and Hananiah, a perfumer, restored the wall to the section known as the "Broad Wall" (v. 8). The remaining builders of the west wall included Rephaiah, Jedaiah, Hattush, Malchijah, Hasshub who repaired both the Tower of the Ovens and another section. Verse 12 states the surprising fact that Shallum put his daughters to work on the west wall.

South wall assignments (3:13-14).—The south wall assignments began with the Valley Gate and extended to the Dung Gate (1,500 ft.). Hanun and the citizens of Zanoah, located over twelve miles west of Bethlehem, did that repair. Malchijah of Bethhaccherem, four miles west of Jerusalem, repaired the Dung Gate. The Dung Gate mentioned in verse 14 is probably the Potsherd Gate of Jeremiah 19:2.

East wall assignments (3:15-32).—The first assignment for the east wall went to Shallum, who rebuilt and repaired the Fountain Gate and the wall of the Pool of Shelah. Nehemiah, son of Azbuk, worked from a point opposite the royal cemetery to the artificial pool and on to the military headquarters ("house of the mighty men"). The "Nehemiah" mentioned above was not the one whose memoirs are recorded in this book. Nehemiah 1:1 lists his father's name as Hacaliah, not Azbuk. The next workers on the east wall included the Levites: Rehum, Hashabiah, Bavvai, Ezer, Baruch, and Meremoth. They were followed by these men, presumed to be priests: Benjamin, Hasshub, Azariah, Binnui, Palal, and Pedaiah. The Tekoites repaired the wall of Ophel. Each of the priests repaired opposite his own home. Zadok, Shemaiah, Hananiah, Hanun, Meshullam, and Malchijah are listed by name as workers.

The goldsmiths and merchants completed the last section. According to verse 32, they joined the wall from the upper chamber to the Sheep Gate (the beginning section of the wall, v. 1), thus completing the circuit of Jerusalem's city wall.

Resolve in the Face of Opposition (4:1-23)

The Chronicler had explained in chapter 3 who had received assignment to work on the city wall and where each person worked. In chapter 4 he returned to a discussion of the opposition encountered in the process of building. Most commentators believe that the Chronicler inserted these verses to explain the delay in completion of the wall and gates.

A continuing opposition (4:1-3).—From the beginning, Sanballat and Tobiah had been hostile towards Nehemiah's return. After they observed the progress of the wall builders, they became even more disturbed. They viewed the rebuilding of the city wall as tangible evidence that Judah's power was on the increase and their own power was on the decrease. Sanballat and Tobiah knew that Nehemiah had the backing of the king. Therefore, they used the only weapon immediately available—destruction of the morale of the workers through ridicule.

Verses 1 and 2 focus on Sanballat's reaction to the wall: "He was angry and greatly enraged, and he ridiculed the Jews" (v. 1). However, along with the anger and ridicule, he apparently tried to evaluate the seriousness of the situation. He conferred with his allies whether these allegedly feeble Jews could actually restore the wall. The possibility of their rebuilding the wall and gates from the rubbish piles seemed unlikely.

Tobiah's reply revealed more sarcasm than honest assessment. His retort that even a fox could "break down their stone wall!" (v. 3) illustrates his ignorance of the true situation. Excavations show that Nehemiah built his wall about nine feet thick. A fox would not likely break down a structure of that strength.

Prayer for vengeance (4:4-5).—News about his enemies' consultation reached Nehemiah. He had a keen awareness of the demoralizing effect that his enemies' taunts had upon the workers. He also felt that his people were doing God's will in rebuilding the city wall. Therefore, he reasoned that the enemies who opposed it stood in opposition to the Lord. On that basis he prayed the prayer for vengeance contained in verses 4-5.

In essence, Nehemiah pled for God to reverse the situation and cause Judah's enemies to be taunted instead of Judah. This plea included a request for the defeat and captivity of his foes. The brief prayer ended with an appeal to God *not* to forgive their sin, implying that the enemies should receive their just punishment. The last clause of verse 5 explains the reason.

Imprecatory prayers (prayers for vengeance) run contrary to the principles of Christ, who taught forgiveness of enemies. This type of prayer seems strange coming from the lips of apparently righteous people. Modern readers can only surmise that Nehemiah lived by the light of his own day. Imprecatory prayers were acceptable by Old Testament standards.

Progress, conspiracy, and self-defense (4:6-18a).—Verse 6 indicates that the work progressed in spite of outside resistance. The people completed half the height of the wall. The last part of verse 6 focuses on the reason for this progress: "The people had a mind to work."

Predictably, Sanballat, Tobiah, and Judah's other enemies became very angry when they heard the report. The repairing of the walls and the closing of the breaches (v. 7) signified that "these feeble Jews" (v. 2) had more power than their foes thought. The enemies therefore plotted together to stop the wall building by making a secret attack on Jerusalem, thereby causing confusion. Meanwhile the people of Judah operated on the principle that God helps those who help themselves. They prayed to God with their lips while they defended themselves physically by posting guards (v. 9). However, verse 10 (originally a poem fragment) indicates that much rubbish from the old wall still remained, and the men who had to carry these materials were physically exhausted.

Judah's enemies may have gotten word of the plight described in verse 10. If so, this information would have increased the effectiveness of their plot. They resolved to keep the actual time of their planned attack so secret that when they struck they would take the Jews by surprise. They would then slay the wall builders.

Jews who lived near Judah's enemies got wind of the plot. The expression, "They said to us ten times" (v. 12) probably refers to a relaying system used in getting the information to the builders. This message prompted Nehemiah to station armed guards at open places at the base of the wall to protect the structure and its builders. He reassured his people of God's help and urged them to defend their fellow Jews and their own families. Evidently the strategy worked. The workmen returned to their job (v. 15). From then on, however, the Jews devised a more effective way of continuing the project. Verse 16 reports that half the workers built while the other half stood guard. A back-up of leaders stood behind all of them. Furthermore, the burden carriers (another class of workers) carried materials in one hand and a weapon in the other. Each of the builders had a sword girded at his side (v. 18a).

Warning and working (4:18b-23).—Verse 18b states that Nehemiah had a trumpeter by his side. The office of trumpeter involved keeping watch over the city in order to warn citizens of impending danger. The sound of the curved horn (trumpet) would signal the workers to gather at a specified place (v. 20). Again Nehemiah assured them of God's protection.

Nehemiah instructed the workers who lived in outlying areas to remain in Jerusalem at night and serve as guards. All the workers, including Nehemiah, literally remained in their work clothes day and night. The words "None of us took off our clothes" (v. 23) imply that they remained ready for action at all times.

The reader might ask: Why the sudden hurry to finish the job after so long a delay? Primarily it was because a completed wall would offer more protection than an unfinished one. The strong leadership of Nehemiah afforded a discipline over the workers not previously attained. Partly, "the people had a mind to work" because Nehemiah would not let them quit. Throughout the building program he constantly observed, prodded, encouraged, led, and joined the workers. The most effective leaders of today still use these methods.

Financial Problems of Judah (5:1-19)

Interpreters differ in their opinions as to whether chapter 5 belongs in its present order in the book. The reason for the question lies in the dating of verse 14 which says that Nehemiah had reigned as governor for twelve years when the financial problem came to light. This was far behind the time of the completion of the city wall. On the other hand, free labor on the wall for an extended period of time would have robbed the workmen of the opportunity for paid employment elsewhere. This factor, too, could have caused financial distress. Therefore, the question remains uncertain as to whether the economic problem described in chapter 5 related to the wall building or to a different cause.

The people's outcry (5:1-5).—Previously, the Jews had aired their grievances against *external* enemies who had scorned them. Chapter 5 mainly records their outcry against wealthy fellow Jews who contributed to, and profited from, their poverty. Verses 1-5 outline the reasons for their complaints.

First, they spoke of the famine that had caused such distress. They had large families and no way to feed them. As a result, they had mortgaged their fields, vineyards, and houses in order to buy grain (v. 3).

Second, they had to borrow money in order to pay their taxes to the king. Their own fellow Jews had become unscrupulous moneylenders. They demanded fields and vineyards as collateral for the loans, knowing that the impoverished Jews would have to surrender their property. Even worse, the moneylenders (members of their own race) had demanded that they surrender their children as slaves when they had no property to give.

Nehemiah's outrage (5:6-13).—Nehemiah reacted with great anger when he heard how the wealthy Jews had treated their impoverished brethren. He privately considered the matter, then confronted the nobles and officials with their sin. The Jews to whom he spoke understood the covenant law forbidding any charge of interest to fellow Jews (Deut. 23:20), yet they did it anyway. Inclusion of the last sentence in verse 7 implies that the guilty persons refused to rectify the situation at first. Nehemiah therefore lined up a large assembly of people and aired the grievances publicly.

Nehemiah reminded his countrymen how they had arranged to return their fellow Jews from exile. He then asked, in effect: Did you provide for their release from foreign slavery only in order to have them enslaved by their fellow countrymen? His question left them speechless (v. 8).

Nehemiah then focused on two fears common to all Jews: (1) punishment from God, and (2) ridicule by other nations. Their evil actions had left them vulnerable on both counts. Actually, God often used national defeat and disgrace as a mode of punishment for his people. Nehemiah called attention to his own practice of lending money to his impoverished fellow Jews without charging interest. He appealed to the nobles and officials not only to lend without interest, as he did, but also to return the property confiscated.

This time the offenders responded positively. In the presence of the priests they took an oath that they would keep their promise. Nehemiah symbolically shook out his "lap" (whose folds served as pockets) to empty it. He declared that if the offenders did not keep their promise, their pockets would be emptied. This statement amounted to the pronouncement of a curse upon them if they did not fulfill their promise. The rest of the large assembly assented with an "Amen" (v. 13).

Nehemiah's conduct in office (5:14-19).—Nehemiah had served as governor for twelve years, having replaced Sanballat. He had governed his people in a righteous manner. Unlike his predecessor, he had refused the food and monetary allowance normally allotted to a governor. He did not want to impose any further burden on his people. Even the servants of the former governor had "lorded it over" the people (v. 15). Nehemiah refused to follow their example. He had also continued to work on the city wall and had acquired no land for himself.

Verse 17 takes further note of Nehemiah's generosity. He had furnished money from his own pocket to pay for the feeding of 150 members of his administrative staff. Food for one day for his staff included an ox and six sheep, fowls, and wine. He did it at his own expense, even though he had the right to exact the cost from those whom he governed.

Chapter 5 concludes with a brief prayer. Nehemiah asked God to remember him. However, he did not ask God to favor him because of his status as governor or his administrative ability but because of his role as servant. His goodness (v. 19) lay in what he did for his fellow Jews. His work would become his memorial. Nehemiah's prayer brings to mind the later words of Jesus: "Whoever would be great . . . must be your slave" (Matt. 20:26-27).

Plots Against Nehemiah (6:1-14)

Chapter 6 picks up at a point where the wall is almost complete. Nevertheless, the attempts to stop the workers, and especially to harass Nehemiah, had by no means ended. Verses 1-14 tell of the plot to ambush Nehemiah and intimidate the workers.

Nehemiah sees through the plot (6:1-4).—The breaches in the wall had already been filled. The workers only lacked the hanging of the doors of the gates before completion of the project. The enemies who had allied themselves against Judah had not been successful in their previous attempts to stop the builders. Their last-ditch efforts were more of an attempt to destroy Nehemiah than to halt progress on the wall.

Sanballat and Geshem, and the other enemies of Judah, sent a message to Nehemiah, inviting him to meet with them for a conference. They selected the plain of Ono (about nineteen miles from Jerusalem) as a neutral place to meet. Nehemiah, however, saw through their plot. He responded with the message: "I am doing a great work and I cannot come down. Why should the work stop while I leave it and come down to you?" (v. 3). The last part of this verse suggests two possible interpretations: (1) Nehemiah's work was too important for him to leave, just in order to have a conference with them; or (2) if they want to have a conference, they can come to him, instead of his coming to them. On four different occasions Nehemiah received a similar invitation, but each time he rejected it.

Another attempt to frighten Nehemiah (6:5-9).—The fifth message that Sanballat sent contained an open threat. The letter accused the Jews of building the wall in preparation for a rebellion against Persia. Sanballat falsely accused Nehemiah of trying to set himself up as king. This charge, if true, would make Nehemiah guilty of treason. Sanballat claimed he had heard the rumor that Nehemiah had appointed prophets to proclaim Nehemiah as the awaited king (a messianic implication). Sanballat threatened to report the matter to the king of Persia.

The rumor, of course, had no basis in fact. Sanballat had simply invented it to frighten the Jews and make them abandon the work on the wall. Nehemiah responded by uttering the prayer: "O God, strengthen thou my hands" (v. 9).

A trick by a false friend (6:10-14).—Sanballat again plotted against Nehemiah, this time by hiring Shemaiah (presumably a prophet or priest) to trick Nehemiah. Shemaiah pretended to offer Nehemiah protection within the closed doors of the Temple. The suggestion involved a subtle attempt to violate religious law. (Laymen and eunuchs could not enter the inner Temple; and Nehemiah was both a layman and a eunuch.) Shemaiah pretended to base his invitation on the claim that Nehemiah's foes planned to attack him. Actually, he hoped to discredit Nehemiah.

Nehemiah saw through the trickery. First, he did not fear the threats of assassination. Second, he respected the religious law that prohibited him from entering a place reserved for priests. Verse 13 records Nehemiah's analysis of the situation. He surmised that his enemies had paid off Shemaiah to tempt him to sin and destroy his good name.

Earlier Nehemiah had prayed that God would remember *him* for his goodness (v. 19). In 6:14 he prayed that God would remember *his enemies* for their evil.

The section "The Rebuilding Program" (1:1 to 6:14) concludes on the note that although Nehemiah faced much opposition, he did not lose courage. He continued to rebuild the wall of protection around Jerusalem.

Completion, Census, and Congregation
6:15 to 8:18

The second section of Nehemiah (6:15 to 8:18) deals primarily with the completion of the wall, the taking of a census, and the gathering of the people to hear Ezra read the law. Nehemiah 7:6-73 contains a long genealogy of Jerusalem's inhabitants, very similar to the one in Ezra 2:3-67. Because of space limitations, the Nehemiah commentary will only refer to the list in a general way. For further information, refer to the commentary on Ezra 2:1-70.

The Wall Completed (6:15-19)

Nehemiah 6:15 gives the startling information that the workers completed the wall of Jerusalem in only fifty-two days—a very short time, considering the magnitude of the task. The reader can only assume that a combination of God's intervening hand and the persistent leadership of Nehemiah enabled the builders to fulfill their mission so quickly. No doubt the pressing need of a protective city wall for defense also served as an incentive to rush the project.

Victory with God's help (6:16).—Predictably, news of the wall's completion deflated the ego of Judah's enemies. Tobiah and the others could no longer view Judah as a defenseless nation, vulnerable to oppression and attack. The perception that Judah had received divine support in the wall building made the situation more threatening. Judah's foes had not just been fighting "feeble Jews" (4:2); they had unknowingly fought God! No wonder that with God's help the Jews had succeeded in rebuilding the wall.

The theme of "victory with God's help" runs throughout the entire Bible. Nehemiah contains one of many biblical illustrations that God helps and supports those who serve him. Nehemiah's enemies had persecuted, threatened, and tried to deceive him in order to put an end to the wall building. Nevertheless, Nehemiah and his fellow Jews managed to complete the wall. The only feasible explanation lies in the statement at the end of verse 16: "This work had been accomplished with the help of our God."

Account of conspiracy (6:17-19).—The Chronicler who compiled Nehemiah's memoirs evidently inserted verses 17-19 here for topical, rather than chronological, reasons. It supports the fact that Nehemiah faced continuous opposition during the building of the city wall. Chronologically, of course, verse 15 had already reported the wall as complete.

Sanballat had previously proved his own inability to stop Nehemiah. Sanballat's ineffectiveness may explain why verses 17-19 place Tobiah in the foreground at this point. These verses also show that Nehemiah did not have the full support of all his fellow Jews.

The nobles of Judah (high officials in Jewish affairs) kept up a correspondence with Tobiah concerning Nehemiah and the wall. They acted as spies within their own nation. They also praised Tobiah in Nehemiah's presence, then reported to Tobiah how he reacted. Tobiah, in turn, sent threatening letters to Nehemiah.

What would prompt these Jewish officials to conspire against Nehemiah, a leader bent only on helping his nation? Verse 18 suggests one of the reasons. Tobiah had married the daughter of Shecaniah (a Jew), and his son had married the daughter of Meshullam (also a Jew). A later passage, 13:28, further notes that Sanballat's daughter had married the chief priest's grandson. Because of these intermarriages, Tobiah and Sanballat had formed friendships with important Jewish families. The Jewish friends were bound by oath to serve Tobiah's and Sanballat's purpose of hindering Nehemiah. The Jewish nobles had likely developed a professional jealousy against Nehemiah because of his success.

Watchmen Appointed (7:1-3)

Chapter 7 resumes the narrative at a point after the completion of the city wall. Hanging of the doors was the last part of the construction. The city wall, includings its door, helped protect the city, but the city also needed additional defense. Therefore, Nehemiah arranged for security guards.

Nehemiah appointed his brother Hanani and the chief of the citadel, Hananiah, faithful and God-fearing men, to officiate over the city. (Some scholars believe that both names referred to the same man.) These officials received instructions not to open the Jerusalem gates until the heat of the day and to close them before the guards went off duty. Nehemiah ordered that the residents of Jerusalem take turns keeping appointed watches at the stations near their own homes. Psychologically, the plan had a sound basis. Citizens would have greater incentive to serve in this way when it involved defending their own homes and neighborhood.

The Census (7:4-73a)

Although Jerusalem was large in area, it had become depopulated after its destruction. Even after their return from the Exile, the Jews had not rebuilt their homes there. Nehemiah knew that

Jerusalem would not become an important and respectable city again until it increased greatly in population.

After prayerful consideration, Nehemiah assembled the people of Judah for a census. He then listed them by families. During the census-taking process, he located a book containing a genealogical list of the early returnees from exile. Verses 7-73a record the family names and number of members registered in that early list. However, verses 61-65 indicate that some of those assembled for the census could not prove their genealogy. Included among them were some priests. The priests received instruction not to partake of the holy food until a priest rose up who could validate them. ("Urim and Thummim," v. 65, refers to the practice of receiving divine affirmation or negation through casting of lots by a priest.)

As indicated earlier, Nehemiah had ordered the census for the purpose of redistributing the population of Judah. Mainly he saw the need to repopulate Jerusalem so that it would regain its former strength. Verse 73 refers to a redistribution but does not state how many people actually moved to Jerusalem.

Congregating to Hear the Law (7:73b to 8:18)

During the seventh month (Sept.-Oct.) the Jews gathered to receive instruction in the Mosaic law. Ezra, the priest-scribe, read and interpreted the law in such a way that his listeners understood the meaning (v. 8). The people showed their respect for God's law by standing attentively while it was read (v. 5).

Verse 9 refers to the weeping of the people during the reading of the scroll. The weeping could have been a sentimental reaction, based on memories of past occasions. More likely, however, it related to repentance for failing to keep the law. Nehemiah and Ezra responded by asserting that they had not gathered the people on that particular day to weep but to rejoice. They instructed the assembly to eat and drink joyfully and to share gifts of food with one another.

The next day the family heads, together with the priests and Levites, gathered to make a further study of the Mosaic law. During the study they discovered instructions for a celebration that they had apparently forgotten, the Feast of Booths. The law set the appointed time for it as the seventh month. Nehemiah 7:73 indicates that it was already the seventh month when they made the discovery. Therefore, the people made preparations to observe this happy time.

In keeping with their instructions the people gathered branches of olive, pine, myrtle, palm, and other leafy trees from which to build the booths. Those who resided in Jerusalem set up booths on their flat rooftops and courts. Presumably the priests and Levites placed booths in the court of the Temple. People who lived outside Jerusalem used the area of the Gate of Ephraim (v. 16). Each day during the celebration Ezra read aloud from the Mosaic law. A solemn assembly followed the seven days of the Feast of Booths. During a holy day, such as the solemn assembly, the people did not work.

Confession and Dedication Ceremonies
9:1 to 12:47

Nehemiah 9:1 to 12:47, the third section of the book, deals mainly with two topics: a day of repentance and confession and the dedication of Jerusalem's wall. This section also provides an answer to a question left unanswered in 7:73: How was the population of Judah redistributed, and, especially, how many people moved to Jerusalem?

The chronology of chapters 9—12 presents somewhat of a problem. Interpreters generally agree that Nehemiah 9 should follow Ezra 10 and that Nehemiah 12:27-43 should follow Nehemiah 11:36. As indicated in the Ezra introduction, the Chronicler interwove parts of the Ezra-Nehemiah material in compiling it. Nevertheless, chapters 9—12 carry an unmistakable message: Confession and repentance are vital in obtaining God's forgiveness and restoration. This ancient principle continues to apply in the Christian era.

Repentance and Reform (9:1 to 10:39)

In Old Testament days a close relation existed between the nation and the individual. If the nation of Judah prospered, the individual shared in the joy of that prosperity. Likewise, if the nation sinned, the individual shared responsibility and punishment for the sin of the nation. Ezra and Nehemiah, although not personally guilty, shared responsibility for Judah's sin and led their nation to repentance and reform.

Nehemiah 9:1-3 relates to the day of penitence observed by the whole nation because of its sin. Verses 4-37 contain the penitential prayer of that occasion. Nehemiah 9:38 to 10:39 deals with the resulting pledge of reform made by the people and contains a list of those who "set their seal" (10:1) on the document.

National repentance (9:1-3).—The people assembled for a day of repentance and fasting on the "twenty-fourth day of this month." This dating indicates that the day of penance closely followed the Feast of Booths (8:18). Assuming the correctness of the dating, a period of rejoicing preceded the day of national repentance—a puzzling arrangement. Also of interest is the fact that at the reading of the law the people had wept, probably because they had not kept the law. At that time Ezra and Nehemiah had instructed them to rejoice, not weep (8:9). Conversely, in 9:1-3, soon after the joyful occasion, the people had obviously received instruction to do the reverse: weep, not rejoice. (Fasting and sackcloth signified repentance and mourning.)

The nation observed the day of mourning, penitence, and confession because of their national sins and those of their ancestors. The people showed their mourning in three ways: fasting, wearing coarse sackcloth, and putting dust on their heads. Furthermore, they excluded all non-Israelites for religious reasons. They stood up to listen to the reading of the Book of the Law and to confess their sins. Those persons not guilty of the sin of their fellow Jews joined in the confession and penitence—another example of how the individual identified with the sin of the nation.

The penitential prayer (9:4-37).—Following the confessional and the reading of the law, the Levites led in a penitential prayer. This lengthy prayer, although addressed to God, encompassed a retelling of Israel's history. It also served the additional purpose of instructing and warning the nation, a technique commonly used.

The prayer contained in these verses actually comes under the heading of a penitential psalm. It consists mainly of indirect quotations from numerous biblical sources. The writer of this psalm-prayer carefully intertwined a wide spectrum of his nation's religious and historic background. Nevertheless, the prayer focuses on God's gracious acts in his people's behalf, not on human accomplishments.

This passage begins with a call to worship, followed by words of praise to God. Verses 6-25 outline the many evidences of God's gracious hand in Israel's history. They include the call of Abraham, the Exodus, divine sustenance and protection during the wilderness journey, and the conquest of Canaan. Verses 26-31 confess the nation's sin in spite of God's graciousness. They broadly define the people's disobedience of God's law and God's punishment of the nation because of its sin. The prayer calls attention to the redemptive forgiveness that always followed the nation's repentance. Verse 31 summarizes the reason for the nation's continued existence up to that time, in spite of a history of sin: "Nevertheless in thy great mercies thou didst not make an end of them or forsake them; for thou art a gracious and merciful God."

God's people deserved the punishment that God inflicted on them in the form of defeat and oppression. (Jews viewed military defeat as divine punishment.) Nevertheless, they again pled that God would pity them in their plight. Their conquerors had demanded the fruit of the fields that God had intended for his people, had taken command of their herds, and had enslaved the people. God's people prayed that God would take their plight seriously and show pity on them again.

A signed pledge (9:38 to 10:39).—In anticipation that God would again show mercy on his people, the princes, Levites, priests, and laymen signed a legal document affirming their pledge of reform. Chapter 10:1-27 contains a list of the signers, headed by Nehemiah (the governor). The document began with a general pledge to obey God's commandments. The words "to enter into a curse and an oath" (v. 29) meant that anyone who made the pledge did so with the knowledge that he could receive punishment if he broke his promise. The chief focus of the pledge related to mixed marriages, a deep concern shared by Ezra (Ezra 9:11-12). Verse 30 relates to that concern.

Verses 31-39 list some other terms of the agreement. (1) The people of Judah would refuse to buy grain on the sabbath or on a holy day. (2) They would let their fields and orchards rest every seventh year. (3) They would not collect repayment for debts the seventh year. (4) They would pay their assessment of one-third shekel (about 12.2 grams) yearly for Temple support. This tax would be used for the "showbread" (bread to show God), cereal offering, burnt offering, supplementary sabbath offerings, new moons, appointed feasts, "holy things" (public offerings), sin offerings, and the Temple upkeep. Verse 34 relates to the practice of bringing wood to assure a perpetual flame on the altar. The people would "cast lots" to determine who could supply the wood at what time. They probably based this practice on Leviticus 6:9.

A further condition of the reform-pledge included bringing the firstfruits of the fields and trees annually to the Temple. Likewise, the people pledged to bring the firstborn of their sons, cattle, herds, floods, fruit, wine, and oil. The law of firstfruits had its source in Exodus 13:2 and 22:29-30. The people also pledged the tithes from the ground to the Levites, who in turn would bring them to the Temple storehouse. (See Lev. 27:30 for the law concerning tithes of the ground.)

The last part of verse 39 reveals the underlying purpose for observing these laws: "We will not neglect the house of our God." This pledge speaks to a need of worshipers of today. At a time when so many apparently "good causes" vie for our financial support, they tend to sidetrack us from supporting God's house. Contributing to the support of charities and civic causes does not relieve us of stewardship responsibility toward God's house. To think otherwise is contrary to the teachings of the Bible (Mal. 3:10).

Repopulating Jerusalem (11:1 to 12:47)

The comments relating to Nehemiah 7:4-73 spoke of the need for a redistribution of the population of Judah. Nehemiah had ordered a census in order to compile a genealogical list of the families of Judah. The ultimate purpose was to determine how to repopulate Jerusalem so that it would again become a powerful city. Chapter 7 did not state how Nehemiah would implement the plan or who actually moved to Jerusalem, however.

Nehemiah 11:1 to 12:47 returns to the plan for repopulating Jerusalem. This passage provides the reader with more details about the endeavor.

The method of choice (11:1-2).—Verse 1 informs us that the leaders already lived in Jerusalem at that time. Obviously the city needed many people besides the leaders and the rest of the current inhabitants in order to populate itself to a respectable size again.

The residents of Judah cast lots to determine who would move to the "holy city" (11:1). Jerusalem originally received its name *Holy City* because of the presence of the "holy of holies" within the Temple.

Casting of lots carried a religious connotation in ancient Judah. Usually a person selected by this method had a sacred duty to abide by the decision, but in this instance there appears to have been an element of voluntary sacrifice. Verse 2 speaks of the fact that "the people blessed all the men who willingly offered to live in Jerusalem." The casting of lots assured that Jerusalem could contain one-tenth of the citizenry of Judah.

List of Jerusalem's residents (11:3 to 12:26).—The list of people who moved to Jerusalem begins in 11:3 with an account of the lay leaders ("chiefs"). Following the lay leaders of verses 3-9, Nehemiah mentioned the priests (vv. 10-14), including three priestly groups: Jedaiah, Jachin, and Seraiah. In verses 15-18 he listed the Levites, again consisting of the families of three Levites (Shemaiah, Mattaniah, and Abda). Verse 18 says that 284 Levites resided in Jerusalem.

The remainder of the list consists of miscellaneous inhabitants: gatekeepers, Temple servants, overseers. Verses 25-36 inform readers that others settled in towns outside of Jerusalem.

Nehemiah 12:1-26 appears to be an appendix that the Chronicler added to the above list. Possibly he did it to provide information about the priests and Levites who officiated during the long Persian period. Verses 10-11 give a genealogy of the post-Exilic priests and verses 12-21 of the priests under Joiakim. Verse 22 concerns the priestly family in the days of Eliashib, while verses 23-26 deal exclusively with the Levites.

Dedicating Jerusalem's walls (12:27-43).—The dedication of the city wall was a joyful occasion. The Levites throughout Judah received a summons to come to Jerusalem and participate in the celebration. Musicians came to praise God with their voices and instruments, including cymbals, harps, and lyres. Part of the ritual consisted of purifying the worshipers, gates, and wall. Priests and Levites performed that function (v. 30).

Verses 31-42 describe the processional at the dedication. One choir group marched upon the wall from the right side. Presumably the other group went from the left. The marching "upon the wall" could be literal, since the wall had a thickness of nine feet. Everyone, including Nehemiah, gave thanks in the Temple courts. The singing, instrumental music, and rejoicing of the worshipers caused the joy of Jerusalem to be heard for a great distance (v. 43).

The giving of sacrifices became the high point of an altogether joyful occasion. The people, and especially Nehemiah, knew that they could not have completed the wall without divine support. An earlier passage (6:16) properly credits the accomplishment to God's help. Appropriately, therefore, the Jewish nation climaxed their celebration with sacrificial offerings to the One who had made possible the rebuilding of Jerusalem's wall of defense (v. 43).

Righteous provision for the Temple (12:44-47).—Although the phrase "on that day" (v. 44) appears, on the surface, to connect this passage with the previous one, it does not necessarily do it. The same term also carried the vague connotation of "later" or "at another time." However, verses 44-47 do give the reader insight about Temple administration under ideal circumstances. The passage provides a basis of contrast between what Temple administration was like ideally, and how it later deteriorated.

Verse 44 illustrates the efficiency of Temple administration in that era. Appointed officials kept the storage chambers filled with sacrificial supplies. Likewise they supervised collection of the contributions, firstfruits, and tithes, and apportioned them among the priests and Levites, as required by law.

The Levites, in turn, performed their duties in a worthy manner (v. 45). In like manner, the singers and gatekeepers carried out their functions well. All the Jews financially supported them. Singers, gatekeepers, Levites, and priests received their portions.

The Reforms of Nehemiah
13:1-31

Nehemiah had served as governor for twelve years during his first administration. The time came for him to return to Persia to report to the king who had so graciously granted his leave from his official post (2:6). The narrative does not say how long he remained in Persia before a return to Jerusalem.

Chapter 13 deals with Nehemiah's second administration as governor of Judah. The chapter relates primarily to his vigorous reforms during that administration. The conditions that Nehemiah found when he returned to Judah contrasted strongly with the ones described earlier.

Tobiah's Expulsion (13:1-9)

Verses 1-3 reveal the basis for exclusion of Ammonites and Moabites from the congregation. During the Exodus these nations had refused to help the Jews in any manner. In fact, they "hired Balaam against them to curse them" (v. 2), but God had turned the curse into a blessing. According to Deuteronomy 23:3-5, this action had resulted in a law that excluded Ammonites and Moabites from the Israelite congregation.

Tobiah was an Ammonite. The law, cited above, provided Nehemiah with a legal right to expel this longtime enemy from the Temple chambers—a right he quickly exercised.

Tobiah's expulsion (13:4-9).—During Nehemiah's absence Tobiah had somehow managed to move into a large chamber of the Temple. The chamber had previously served as a storage space for Temple supplies. Verse 4 lays the blame for Tobiah's presence on Eliashib, a priest who had some sort of kinship to Tobiah (probably by marriage). When Nehemiah returned to Jerusalem and discovered Tobiah's residence at the Temple, he became incensed. He threw all of Tobiah's household furniture out of the chamber, then ordered a ritual cleansing of the area that had become religiously polluted by Tobiah's presence. After the cleansing, Nehemiah brought back the vessels, cereal offering, and frankincense formerly stored there (v. 9).

Restoring Support for the Levites (13:10-14)

Upon his return, Nehemiah also found that the Levites and singers had not received payment during his absence. Lack of support had forced them to return to their farms to live. Nehemiah confronted the officials with what had happened, accusing them of letting God's house be forsaken through neglect of their duty.

Nehemiah then restored the Levites to their position at the Temple. Judah resumed the practice of bringing their tithe of grain, wine, and oil, from which the Levites would receive payment. Furthermore, Nehemiah appointed new treasurers over the storehouses, men who would administer faithfully.

Following the reform, Nehemiah prayed: "Remember me, O my God, concerning this, and wipe not out my good deeds that I have done for the house of my God and for his service" (v. 14). Here Nehemiah reflected the ancient view that God literally wrote down all of men's good and evil deeds. He wanted God to credit to his account what he had done for God's house and its service.

Sabbath Reforms (13:15-22)

Sabbath observance had deep roots in the religious history of Israel. It signified faithfulness to Yahweh, distinguished Israel's religion from that of neighboring nations, and fulfilled God's command (Ex. 20:8). Nevertheless, Jewish religious history shows that the nation did violate the sabbath many times. The prophets had to warn their people repeatedly of the serious consequences of sabbath breaking (Jer. 17:27; Ezek. 20:13; 22:8-9; Amos 3:5).

Nehemiah 13:15-22 describes Nehemiah's consternation when he saw people boldly disregarding the sabbath. He found men using winepresses, carrying and loading grain, wine, grapes, figs, and other burdens. The men intended to bring these farm products into Jerusalem for sale (v. 15). Fishermen from Tyre likewise brought fish and other wares to Jerusalem on the sabbath. Jews bought these supplies from the vendors, knowing that they transgressed sabbath law by so doing.

Sabbath observance renewed (13:17-22).—Again Nehemiah held the secular officials of Judah responsible for the situation he found. He warned them that they had increased God's wrath against Judah by allowing the sabbath to be profaned. He then ordered that the gatekeepers shut the city gates before dark, prior to the sabbath, and leave them closed until the sabbath ended. He placed watchmen over the gates to make sure that the vendors could not enter. In spite of Nehemiah's warning, the vendors camped outside the gates, probably hoping to smuggle their goods inside. This time Nehemiah threatened them. His threat evidently worked, because verse 21 states that they stopped coming on the sabbath. The Levites ritually cleansed themselves and resumed their sabbath posts at the gates.

This section ends with another request for God to remember how Nehemiah restored holiness to the sabbath. However, he based his prayer on God's steadfast love, not his own merits (v. 22).

Mixed Marriage Reforms (13:23-29)

Another problem that had cropped up frequently during Jewish history related to intermarriage of Jews with foreigners. Mixed marriages always increased the risk that men of the Jewish faith might either adopt the religion of their wives or compromise their own religion with pagan practices. That danger explains why both Ezra and Nehemiah took such strong stands against mixed marriages.

Nehemiah's violent reaction (13:23-29).—Verse 24 implies that the problem Nehemiah "saw" (v. 23) had existed for a long time. Half of the children of the Jews did not even speak the Jewish language. Instead they spoke the language of Ashdod. Naturally, the children had picked up this language from their foreign mothers. Nehemiah viewed the Hebrew language as a vital sign of Judah's national identity and therefore insisted on keeping it alive. Of far more importance than the language problem, however, was what precipitated it. The Jews had married foreign wives! Their intermarriage violated a commandment God gave them before they entered their Promised Land (Deut. 7:1-3). This breach helps explain the violent behavior of Nehemiah recorded in verse 25.

Nehemiah confronted the guilty men with a considerably stronger appeal than mere "sweet reasoning." He cursed them, beat them, and pulled out their hair (v. 25). In addition, he made them swear that they would not allow their Jewish children to marry foreigners or personally take foreign wives. Nehemiah reminded the transgressors that even a great king like Solomon was accounted guilty because of his association with foreign women. Did Judah want to enrage God by breaking the law concerning mixed marriages?

Although Nehemiah condemned all the Jewish men who had intermarried, he only cited one by name as a notorious example. The grandson of high priest Eliashib had married the daughter of his old enemy, Sanballat (a Horonite). This union could have led to the potential danger of the offspring of a foreign mother succeeding to the office of high priest. Nehemiah chased the offender from Jerusalem (v. 28).

Verse 29 contains another of Nehemiah's appeals to God to remember an incident—this time, however, for the purpose of invoking evil. Eliashib's family members had defiled the priesthood through intermarriage. Nehemiah prayed that God would not forget their sin.

Summary of Reforms (13:30-31)

The memoirs of Nehemiah conclude with a terse summary of what Nehemiah accomplished during this administration as governor. He had rid Judah of foreign influence from mixed marriages (at least temporarily), but especially he had purified the priesthood. He had restored the priests and Levites to their proper function. He had also made provision for the renewal of wood offering and firstfruits at the appointed times. These reforms gave him the right to ask God again to "remember me . . . for good" (v. 31).

Most people continue to remember Nehemiah best for his zeal and leadership in rebuilding the wall of Jerusalem. Figuratively, however, he had also overcome other walls—walls of foreign interference, persecution, apathy and rebellion among his own people, and, finally, backsliding during his absence. In spite of all these challenging walls, Nehemiah succeeded in the task God had called him to do. The city wall he built and the reforms he accomplished increased the national and spiritual strength of his people.

Every generation needs dedicated leaders who are willing to scale challenging walls of opposition, if need be, to carry out God's will. Only as godly people remain alert to the need for reforms can their nations remain spiritually strong.

ESTHER

Introduction

How can a book that does not mention the name of God even once become a canonized part of the Bible? This and other questions concerning the Book of Esther have puzzled scholars through the centuries. Nevertheless, the Jewish Council of Jamnia accepted it in AD 90, and the Council of Carthage accepted it as part of the Christian Bible in AD 397. Since then it has become a favorite book among Jewish persons and an intriguing, even though puzzling, book to Christian readers.

In addition to its failure to mention God's name, Esther also has other controversial features. For example, the book has only two religious or moral teachings: (1) the implied doctrine of Israel as a chosen and indomitable people; and (2) the belief that justice will eventually prevail. Furthermore, Dead Sea Scrolls include material from every other Old Testament book except Esther. Likewise, the New Testament makes no mention of Esther. Another puzzling matter concerns the chief purpose of the book, that of serving as the basis for the celebration of Purim, the only secular "holiday" in the Jewish calendar. (Technically, Jewish leaders do not consider Purim a "holy day" since it does not relate to worship.) The Book of Esther contains the command to all Jews to celebrate on the fourteenth and fifteenth day of the month Adar (Feb.-Mar.) "as the days on which the Jews got relief from their enemies" (Esther 9:22). Today Jews celebrate with merrymaking, giving of gifts, and enactment of the story of Esther.

The dating and authorship of Esther pose a further controversial problem. In broad terms the book likely took shape sometime between the fourth and second century BC. Some historians date it between 165 and 125 BC (Judas Maccabeus' time). Others believe that it came at the end of the Persian period. Most likely, King Ahasuerus (an important character in Esther) was actually Xerxes I. The authorship remains in question. Some commentators believe that either Ezra or Mordecai wrote the book. The author may have been a Persian Jew who had learned about Purim elsewhere and wanted to institute it in Persia.

In spite of the puzzling problems that surround Esther, the book has a valuable contribution to make. It provides information and insights that enhance our understanding of Jewish communal life. It illustrates Israel's ability to survive and even flourish under dangerous conditions. It serves as an example and a source of encouragement to Jews of other generations. It describes interesting customs of Persian court life. It supports secular historical accounts about Xerxes, a Persian ruler. From a literary standpoint, the book has an aura of excitement and intrigue that makes it very readable for Jews and Christians alike.

A circumspect reader would have to admit, however, that Esther's popularity still stems mainly from its relation to the Feast of Purim. Through the centuries the festive celebration of Purim has provided a respite from some of the harsh realities of Jewish life, especially in early Israelite existence. Celebration of Purim prompted a rabbi of AD 300 to say that Esther stands next to the Torah in veneration—a high compliment, considering Jewish respect for the Torah. Jews of today still love the Book of Esther.

The King's Decree
1:1-22

The Book of Esther (the basis of the Feast of Purim) presents many problems. The introduction to this commentary on the book points out a few of them, including the lack of any direct reference to God. In spite of its controversial nature, however, Esther remains one of the most fascinating books in the Bible. History, romance, and adventure race across its pages in quick succession. Readers may recoil at times because of some of the ethics and concepts of justice reflected in Esther, but they will not likely be bored by this extraordinary story.

A Royal Feast (1:1-9)

The book opens by identifying the time and setting of the events of the narrative. The King James Version begins with the words, "Now it came to pass"—an expression that usually indicates a historic event. However, the Revised Standard Version omits these words, apparently interpreting them, in this case, as a mere formula to begin the book. Bible scholars differ in their view as to whether the author of Esther intended the book to be read as history.

King Ahasuerus reigned over the Persian Empire during the time described in Esther. Historians believe that "Ahasuerus" was Xerxes (485-464 BC). His empire included over 127 provinces in an area that extended from India to Ethiopia (1:1). He resided in the city of Susa.

The occasion (1:3-8).—In the third year of Ahasuerus' reign he gave a spectacular banquet for his court, army chiefs, nobles, and governors of the provinces. The banquet lasted for 180 days (half a year). Afterwards King Ahasuerus gave another banquet for all the people in Susa. It lasted seven days. Verses 6-8 describe the lavish nature of the entertainment in detail, including the serving of wine in golden goblets. However, verse 8 notes that the king did not compel any man to drink. Each man could make his own choice in the matter.

The queen's banquet (1:9).—At the same time that King Ahasuerus entertained the men with a banquet, Queen Vashti entertained the women. The separate banquets suggest segregation, but Persian custom did not demand it. Actually, this practice reflected Jewish, rather than Persian, tradition.

Queen Vashti Replaced (1:10-22)

On the seventh day of the banquet the king had become drunk. He commanded his eunuchs (custodians of the women of Persian courts) to bring Queen Vashti to him so that he could show her off. Verse 11 suggests that she had great beauty, especially in royal attire.

For a reason not explained to the reader, Vashti refused to come. The enraged king turned to his "wise men" (in this case, legal experts) for advice on what legal action he should take. The immediate concern of the experts related to how Vashti's actions would affect other women. These experts feared that other women of

Persia and Media would laugh at the king because he could not control Vashti. They therefore recommended that the king replace Vashti with a better queen. They calculated that this move would cause women throughout the kingdom to show greater honor toward their husbands. The king agreed. He sent letters to every province in its own language to notify his subjects that every man should be lord in his own house. The meaning of the last part of 1:22 is not clear. "Speak according to the language of his people" may simply mean that the wife (if foreign) must speak in her husband's language. On the other hand, it may mean that the husband has the right to have the last word.

Esther: The New Queen
2:1-23

Chapter 2 introduces its readers to several elements in the story that may at first seem disconnected. It describes the search to find a new queen to replace Vashti, Mordecai's background and his relationship to Esther, the choice of Esther as queen, and a plot against the king's life. Later, readers will understand why the writer wanted them to know about these events and their background.

Parade of Beautiful Women (2:1-4)

Verse 1 implies that King Ahasuerus may have had second thoughts about what he had done in a drunken rage. The punishment he had ordered for Vashti neither equaled nor fit the crime. However, the original logic behind his decision to depose his queen may have been as follows: If Vashti refuses to appear before me when *I* beckon, then I will make it impossible for her to appear before me when *she* beckons.

The search begun (2:2-4).—If the king felt remorse, as verse 1 seems to indicate, he recovered quickly. His servants lifted his spirits when they suggested beginning a search throughout the kingdom to gather beautiful women. The king's servants advised him to appoint officers in each province to gather these young women and bring them to the palace. These women would remain in the custody of the king's eunuch while they prepared for presentation before the king. They would then appear before the king, and he would choose his favorite as queen. Verse 4 makes it clear that the king liked the plan. He therefore acted on their suggestion for the women to appear before him.

Verses 2-4 reveal an ironic twist to the situation. The king's servants had found an added way in which the rebuffed king could avenge himself and prove his authority. Queen Vashti had refused to parade before him and his friends. Therefore, instead of having only one woman parade before him, he would have all the beautiful young virgins in his kingdom at his beck and call!

(Note: The rule of this king extended to people of non-Persian background, as indicated in 1:1. The king's decision to gather virgins from *every* province for the purpose of selecting a wife conflicts with the Persian historic custom that the king could only marry a Persian.)

Background of Mordecai and Esther (2:5-11)

In verses 5-11 the writer paused in his narrative to give some sketchy background information about two persons. These persons would assume an important role later in the narrative.

Mordecai and Esther (2:5-7).—The writer spoke briefly here about Mordecai, a Jew from the tribe of Benjamin, who had left Jerusalem in the deportation of 597 BC. This may be the same Mordecai mentioned in Ezra 2:2 and Nehemiah 7:7. He resided in Susa at the time of the events recorded in Esther. Mordecai probably held some type of minor position in the government. As the introduction to Ezra in this volume explains, the Babylonians deported the best of Judah's leadership and used these leaders to good advantage during the Exile.

Mordecai had adopted his young cousin, Esther (Hadassah), whose parents had both died. He treated her as a father would treat his own daughter. Mordecai followed the Jewish tradition of relatives taking care of their own kinfolk, especially in the case of orphans and widows.

The author likely inserted the information about Mordecai and his relationship to Esther because it had a significant bearing on what he was about to tell. He wanted his readers to know the unusual circumstances in which the events took place. The story also reveals the unexpected way God worked in behalf of his chosen people.

Esther favored by Hegai (2:8-11).—Verse 8 picks up the main thread of the story again. The king's officers brought many beautiful maidens to the palace, as ordered. Esther quickly gained the favor of Hegai (the one in charge of the women). She received the best place in the harem, as well as ointments, food, and seven maids from the king's house to attend her during her twelve-month beauty program described in verse 12. Verses 8-9 clearly imply that Hegai considered her the most likely choice to fill Queen Vashti's place.

Mordecai had instructed Esther in advance not to reveal her Jewish identity or her relationship to him. The writer did not explain why. Presumably it related to prejudice between Jews and Persians. The narrative gives no reason to believe that Esther refused nonkosher food or followed other Jewish regulations during that time. In the meanwhile Mordecai checked on her daily to see how she fared (2:11).

King's Selection of Esther (2:12-23)

After the twelve-month beautification program, each woman appeared before the king. Individually, the women received whatever they requested to take back to the harem after their appearance before the king. They could not return to the king's house unless the king requested it.

Esther used good strategy in winning the king's approval. She followed Hegai's advice and asked for nothing except what Hegai told her to request. She found favor in the sight of all, but especially the king. He made Esther queen in the seventh year of his reign, four years after he deposed Queen Vashti. The king held a great feast in celebration of Esther's crowning. Even then, Esther did not reveal her Jewish identity.

After Esther became queen, she learned from Mordecai that two of the king's eunuchs had a plot to kill King Ahasuerus. Esther reported it to the king, making sure he knew that Mordecai had provided the information. Naturally, Mordecai's apparent loyalty to the king put Mordecai in good standing with him. The king ordered that the traitors be executed by hanging. He included Mordecai's name in the "Book of the Chronicles" because he had helped the king.

Haman's Promotion and Edict
3:1-15

The next event portrays the traditional hostility between Jews and Amalekites. Mordecai was a Jew and Haman an Amalekite descendant. ("Agagite," v. 1, indicates descendancy from King Agag of Amalek.) Therefore, when the king promoted Haman to grand vizier (a high office) he set the machinery in motion for a real feud.

Haman's Anger (3:1-11)

After his promotion, Haman received great respect from the king's servants, but Mordecai refused to bow down to him. Mordecai remained adamant when the king's servants reprimanded him. Eventually the servants reported this matter to Haman, who angrily decided to kill all the Jews in the kingdom as revenge. His knowledge of Mordecai's Jewish identity, plus his hatred of *all* Jews, prompted the resolve.

Verses 7-11 describe the strategy used by Haman to carry out his resolve. He cast lots ("Pur") to determine when to order the slaughter. Apparently he concluded he should do it on the thirteenth day (unlucky day, vv. 12-13) of the month "Adar." Haman told the king that the people of one of the conquered nations were scattered throughout the provinces. He did not identify the nation as Israel, but this was the nation to which he referred. Haman added that this people's laws differed from the king's laws and that they refused to obey Persian law. He advised the king not to tolerate this conduct.

Still without identifying the name of the people, Haman recommended that the king destroy them (v. 9). Haman offered to pay into the king's treasury ten thousand talents of silver as a bribe for hiring the slaughter of the Jews. (This allotment amounted to nearly two-thirds of the annual income of the Persian empire!) The king accepted Haman's advice (v. 11).

Notifying the Officials (3:12-15)

The king's scribes wrote the edict and sent them to the high officials of every province in the empire. The edict spared no Jew, including the elderly, small children, and women. The king and Haman then sat down and had a drink together. Meanwhile, the edict shocked the citizens of Susa, even though the residents consisted mostly of Gentiles.

Plan to Intercede
4:1 to 5:14

The introduction to this commentary on Esther mentions the nonreligious character of the book. However, chapter 4 does refer to a religious ritual in describing the Jewish reaction to the edict of the king.

Esther's Distress About the Plot (4:1-9)

When Mordecai heard about the edict against Jews, he responded by mourning in the fashion prescribed by Jewish custom. He tore his clothes, put on sackcloth, covered his head with ashes, and wailed loudly. Jews in every province responded the same way. The religious purpose of this mourning ritual was to implore God to intercede in behalf of the Jews. In Mordecai's case it also drew the attention of Esther, so that she would know what had happened.

Esther learned of Mordecai's conduct from her maids and eunuchs. Not understanding the reason for Mordecai's appearance, she sent garments to him, but he would not accept them. She then sent one of the king's eunuchs to investigate what had happened. The eunuch returned with the message that Haman planned to slaughter all the Jews in the empire. Mordecai wanted Esther to intercede with the king in behalf of her fellow Jews. He sent her a copy of the decree for this massacre.

Further Exchange of Messages (4:10-17)

Esther knew that by custom the king's guards would kill anyone who came into the inner court uninvited to approach the king. Only those to whom the king held out his golden scepter would live. The king had not called Esther during the thirty days that had passed thus far. Esther feared for her life if she obeyed Mordecai's order and went to the king uninvited to intercede for the Jews.

When Mordecai learned of her fear, he reminded her that if the decree were carried out, she would not escape any more than the other Jews. Esther's royal status would not help her. If Esther kept quiet about the decree to assassinate all Jews, deliverance of the Jews would come from another source. In that case Esther and her father's house would perish. The phrase "another quarter" (v. 14) apparently implies that God would find another instrument to save his people if Esther refused to do it. The last part of the verse contains the most famous quotation in the book: "Who knows whether you have not come to the kingdom for such a time as this?" This question suggests that God had allowed Esther to become queen of Persia in order that she could save the Jews from destruction.

Esther responded by sending the message to Mordecai that she would do what he had requested. Even though she knew that the mission was illegal, she would take the chance. She said, "If I perish, I perish" (v. 16). However, Esther did ask Mordecai and the other Jews in Susa to fast for three days, a request to which he agreed. Esther and her maids did likewise.

Esther's First Request (5:1-8)

After the three-day fast, Esther donned her royal attire and entered the inner court of the palace. When the king saw Esther, he held out his scepter to indicate that he would allow her to approach him. Surprisingly, the writer made no comment about the relief Esther surely felt at the king's acceptance. The next few verses tell of Esther's strategy in carrying out her mission.

The king knew that Esther would not have risked coming into his presence uninvited without good reason. His offer of half his kingdom in verse 3 was simply a polite Oriental expression, not a literal offer. It meant that he would grant her petition.

Instead of immediately interceding for her people, Esther invited the king and Haman to a banquet she had prepared for them. King Ahasuerus sent a servant to bring Haman there immediately. While drinking wine with Haman, the king again asked about Esther's request. Esther once more postponed telling the king her real request. Instead she repeated the invitation to the king and Haman to come to another banquet the next day. She said that she would make her petition at the banquet.

Haman's False Security (5:9-14)

Esther's invitation to Haman flattered him and put him in a good mood. Haman had not recognized Esther's real motive in the invitation: to lull him into a false sense of security.

Verse 9 tells the reader that Haman had gone on his way in a joyful mood, but when he saw Mordecai at the king's gate, he became angry. Mordecai had refused to acknowledge Haman's position and show proper respect. At that point, however, Haman did not retaliate.

When Haman arrived home, he bragged to his family and friends about his riches, his many children (sign of favor), and his promotion to the office of grand vizier. He then boasted of his invitation from Queen Esther to join the king for a banquet prepared by her. No one but Haman and the king had received this great honor (v. 12).

In spite of these honors, Haman still resented Mordecai's refusal to acknowledge him. Mordecai had spoiled Haman's glorious day by his act of disrespect. Haman told his family that the banquet would do him no good if he had to see Mordecai the Jew when he passed by the king's gate.

Haman's wife and friends devised a solution. They told him to build a spectacular gallows fifty cubits (83 ft.) high. Before the banquet, he could arrange for Mordecai to be hanged there; then he would be able to enjoy the banquet. Verse 14 says that Haman liked their advice and that he proceeded to have the gallows built.

King's Honor of Mordecai

6:1 to 7:10

On the night preceding the banquet the king had trouble going to sleep. He asked his servants to bring the "book of memorable deeds" (v. 1) and read it to him. He listened to the part about how Mordecai had saved his life by informing on two eunuchs who had plotted to kill him. The king asked what honor Mordecai had received for saving his life. He learned that Mordecai had received no honor for doing it.

Mordecai's Deed Rewarded (6:4-11)

By coincidence King Ahasuerus heard Haman in the outer court at about that time. He decided to invite him in and ask: "What should be done to the man whom the king delights to honor?" (v. 6). Haman naturally supposed the king referred to him. He therefore suggested that the king give him a royal robe and a horse previously used by the king. The royal crown (v. 7) would be set on the head of the horse (a Persian custom among royalty). Haman further suggested that the king's most noble prince should array the honoree. The prince could then parade him on horseback through the streets, proclaiming that the king had honored this man.

Haman must have experienced quite a shock when the king revealed the name of the honoree (v. 10). However, he had no choice but to do for Mordecai what he thought would be done for himself. Haman had to go through the humiliating experience of publicly rewarding Mordecai for his good deed in behalf of the king.

Haman's Distress (6:12-14)

After the public ceremony Mordecai returned to the king's gate, but Haman hurried home in great despair. He reported to his wife and friends what had happened. They gave him little comfort. They told him that if Mordecai were indeed a Jew, as Haman had indicated earlier, Haman would surely perish. This prediction refers to the ancient Benjaminite curse against Amalek. (See 1 Sam. 15:3-9.) We have already noted in 3:1 that Haman came from an Amalekite ("Agagite") line. Jewish law had put a curse on the

Amalekites long before then. Haman's friends interpreted Haman's current setback as a bad omen. They gave him no support or encouragement, even though they had contributed to his predicament.

Apparently in Persia, as in Israel, a host customarily sent his servants to bring his guests when the banquet was ready. Verse 14 says that while Haman and his friends discussed the matter, the king's eunuchs arrived to escort Haman to the banquet. Haman had previously faced only humiliation. His most serious trouble lay ahead.

Esther's Petition (7:1-6)

The king and Haman feasted with Queen Esther as planned. The king asked Esther again about the request she wished to make. Esther could no longer postpone answering the king's question. Verses 3-6 bring us to the most dramatic moment in the Book of Esther—the revealing of Esther's request and the undoing of Haman.

Previously Esther had not revealed her identity as a Jewess to the king. In verse 3 she put her life on the line by identifying herself for the first time with those whose lives were in great danger. She petitioned the king to spare both her own life and the lives of her fellow Jews.

Esther then explained the reason for her petition. "We are sold" (v. 4) refers to the bribe Haman offered the king to decree the death of the Jews. She assured the king that if she and her people had merely been sold to the king as slaves, she would have remained silent. Under those circumstances she and her fellow Jews would have willingly accepted their affliction in order to prevent the king's financial loss. "The loss to the king" (v. 4) probably refers to the fact that Haman had planned to pay the king the ten-thousand-talent bribe with money obtained by confiscating the property of slain Jews.

Although the king had previously agreed to Haman's decree, he had not known the true facts or the identity of the people whom Haman wanted massacred. Haman had only told him that "certain people" had refused to obey the king's laws and should be destroyed. (See 3:8.) The king did not know that Haman had trumped up the charges, that the people were Jews, or that Queen Esther was also a Jew. Therefore, the king's question in verse 5 reflects neither

hypocrisy nor forgetfulness. The king really wanted to know who
had ordered such a despicable deed as the destruction of the queen
and her people.

The moment of truth had come. The queen answered with great
drama: "A foe and enemy! This wicked Haman!" (v. 6). Haman
reacted in terror, not knowing what the king would do to him for his
unconscionable act.

Haman's Execution (7:7-10)

After Esther's shocking announcement, the king angrily rose from
the banquet table and walked into the palace garden. He probably
wanted to decide what action to take against this man whom he had
blindly trusted and honored. Meanwhile Haman remained with
Queen Esther, imploring her to intercede for him. In begging
Esther for his life, Haman followed the Persian custom of seizing her
feet while he begged for mercy. Since Esther had been dining, she
was still in a reclining position when Haman seized her feet.
(Persians reclined when they ate.)

When the king returned to the banquet room, he saw Haman in
that position and thought Haman had attacked the queen in his own
house. Esther said nothing to clear up the misunderstanding.
Immediately the king's eunuchs covered Haman's face—a sign that
Haman was destined for execution. One of the eunuchs then told
the king of Haman's plot to hang Mordecai (the king's benefactor) on
the immense gallows he had ordered constructed for that purpose.
This information gave the king the impetus to execute Haman
without further investigation. The king said, "Hang him on that"
(v. 10). Ironically, therefore, Haman hung on the gallows he had
made for Mordecai. The king's anger abated after Haman's execution.

Jews Given Their Revenge
8:1-17

According to Persian law, the state could seize the property of
executed criminals. Chapter 8 illustrates how the king exercised this

right. King Ahasuerus gave Haman's property to Esther. He gave Mordecai (whom he presumably knew by then to be Esther's foster father) the signet ring he had given Haman earlier. This act signified the king's empowerment of Mordecai to use the king's seal as he wished. Mordecai became grand vizier in Haman's place.

Esther's Courageous Intercession (8:1-6)

Already the king had executed Haman, compensated Esther, and promoted Mordecai to grand vizier. However, he had still done nothing about the basic issue, the decree Haman had sent out to slaughter all the Jews. The Jews remained in mortal danger because of this decree. Thus, Esther again had to put her life on the line by appearing before the king when he had not called for her (an offense potentially punishable by death). After the king extended his scepter toward her as a sign of acceptance, he listened to her impassioned plea (v. 4).

Esther went through a polite ritual, as she had earlier, then told the king her petition. She wanted the king to revoke the letters that Haman had written. These letters contained an order to destroy the Jews in all the provinces of the king. Esther said she could not endure the prospects of what would happen to her people if the king did not revoke the orders.

King's New Edict (8:7-14)

The king could not revoke the former decree because of a Persian law that forbade it. (See 1:19.) However, he could serve the same purpose by letting Mordecai write a new decree that counteracted the first one. The king gave Mordecai a free hand, allowing him to write as he pleased and seal it with the king's ring.

For a reason not explained by the writer, Mordecai did not summon the king's secretaries until two months and ten days after Haman's execution (the twenty-third day of Sivan). At that time Mordecai sent a decree to all the high officials of the provinces. The decree permitted the Jews to defend and avenge themselves against their enemies and to plunder their enemies' goods (v. 11). Verse 14 picturesquely speaks of couriers mounted on swift horses, dispatching the new decree. (Note: The KJV translates "horses" as "mules and camels" in v. 14.)

Mordecai's Promotion Made Public (8:15-17)

King Ahasuerus had already privately made Mordecai the new grand vizier, but verse 15 speaks of Mordecai's first public appearance in that office. He wore royal robes of blue and white, a large crown, and a mantle of white and purple (similar to the king's apparel). Earlier when Haman had received appointment as grand vizier, the people had registered a negative type of surprise (3:15). In contrast, according to verse 15, the people rejoiced when Mordecai became grand vizier. Verse 16 describes the Jewish reaction as one of light (symbolizing well-being and prosperity), gladness instead of sadness, joy, and honor.

Everywhere throughout the Persian Empire, the Jews rejoiced over the new decree. They celebrated with a feast and a holiday. So completely had the political tables turned that many Gentiles became Jewish proselytes because they feared Jewish revenge (v. 17).

Destruction and Feast
9:1-32

Chapter 9 shows that those Gentiles who embraced Judaism for political reasons had achieved their purpose. The bloody revenge described in this chapter reveals a merciless slaughter of all the Gentiles suspected of being enemies. The Jews could hardly have needed to slay seventy-five thousand Gentiles merely to protect themselves. The fact that they did not lay their hands on the plunder of their enemies after killing them would not be impressive by Christian standards. However, ancient Jews would have considered this restraint as a sign that they acted only in self-defense.

Jews' Destruction of Enemies (9:1-19)

Originally Haman had selected the thirteenth day of Adar as the time specified to massacre all the Jews (3:13). The choice of the thirteenth day reflected the view of thirteen as an unlucky number.

According to 9:1, the thirteenth day changed from being unlucky for the Jews to unlucky for the Gentiles. The Jews selected that day to gather and slay their enemies.

Due to Mordecai's great power, the various Gentiles who ruled throughout the Persian Empire became turncoats against their own people. They feared that Mordecai would kill them otherwise (vv. 3-4).

Verses 5-11 contain a list of the enemies massacred by the Jews that day. The Jews killed five hundred men in Susa, including the ten sons of Haman. (As mentioned earlier, when the Jews killed their enemies they did not rob them—v. 10.) Still not satisfied with the revenge, Esther requested that the king command that the dead bodies of Haman's sons be hung on the gallows as a means of further disgrace (v. 13).

The Jews who resided in Susa slew three hundred men there on the fourteenth day of Adar (v. 15). Other Jews throughout the king's provinces slew seventy-five thousand enemies but did it on the thirteenth day (vv. 16-17). The dates of the massacres help to explain why the Jews from Susa celebrated with a feast on the thirteenth, whereas the Jews throughout the provinces celebrated on the fourteenth. (See the next section for a further discussion of the celebrations and their respective dates.)

Origin of the Feast of Purim (9:20-32)

The writer of Esther had finally brought the reader to the point for which he wrote the book: the origin of the Feast of Purim. Intriguing though they may have been, chapters 1—8 only provided a literary diversion. The defeat of the enemy (vv. 1-6) brought the narrative to a climax and revealed the reason for the celebration of Purim, a beloved Jewish holiday.

Verse 20 states that Mordecai wrote letters to all the Jews throughout the king's provinces. In these letters he authorized the permanent establishment of the fourteenth and fifteenth days of Adar as festal times for the Jews. Mordecai instructed the Jews to memorialize those days as the time in which sorrow turned into joy for the Jews. In addition to feasting and having a happy celebration, the Jews were to exchange gifts with each other and give gifts to the poor.

Actually, the Jews had already begun their own celebration of victory before they heard Mordecai's order (vv. 17-18). However, Mordecai made the feast days official. The celebration had resulted from the defeat of Haman, a descendant of their historic enemies, the Amalekites.

Verses 24-26 contain a brief summary of the reason for, and origin of, the Jewish festival of Purim. Haman, enemy of the Jews, had cast Pur (lots) in a plot to destroy the Jews. Queen Esther had thwarted the plot by interceding with the king in behalf of her people. As a result, Haman and his ten sons had been hung on the gallows intended for Esther's cousin, Mordecai. In celebrating the event, the Jews called the feast day Purim, after the term *Pur*. They established Purim as a holiday to be observed permanently.

Reference to the "second letter" (v. 29) poses a problem but may refer to a letter written by Esther to support Mordecai's official letter about the feast. Jews throughout all the king's provinces received the letter enjoining them to perpetuate the Feast of Purim. Esther instituted the observance of Purim and had it recorded in writing (v. 32).

Appendix of Book
10:1-3

The author added three verses at the end of the book to underscore the greatness of Mordecai. The book carries the name Esther now, but Mordecai, not Esther, received the real credit for helping the Jews. To a large extent Esther acted under the direction of Mordecai. As grand vizier, Mordecai ranked second only to the king. Verse 2 links Mordecai's name with that of King Ahasuerus (Xerxes). The "Book of the Chronicles of the kings of Media and Persia" referred to in verse 2 may be a historical account of Persian kings written from the Jewish perspective. It might also be an official record in the Persian annals. In addition to Mordecai's official prestige, he had great popularity with the Jews throughout the empire. Mordecai truly cared about the welfare of his fellow Jews.

Earlier we noted that the Book of Esther does not even mention the word *God*. Further, it serves as the basis of a secular celebration, Purim. By Christian standards the book seems quite spiritually unenlightened. Nevertheless, Esther contains Old Testament theological concepts that reveal it is not as godless as it first appears. For example, fasting and mourning, belief in the victory of righteousness over evil, and certainty of Israel's role as God's Chosen People are religious concepts in Judaism. Even the pre-Christian idea of retaliation in kind does not conflict with the "eye for eye" teaching in Exodus 21:24. Esther does bring to the Christian's mind, however, the difference that Christ's coming on earth has made in our understanding of God's purpose and will.

Readers can appreciate Esther for its colorful view of Jewish existence in Persia during the reign of Ahasuerus (Xerxes). In spite of the book's limited spiritual scope, it has a contribution to make. It increases our understanding of the courage and ingenuity required of the Jews just in order to survive in such a perilous period of their history. More than that, however, Esther reveals the greatness of God who quietly worked to deliver his Chosen People.

JOB

Introduction

The Book of Job, a masterpiece of ancient writing, is a rich example of the type of Scripture known as "Wisdom Literature." Like most Wisdom Literature, Job consists of the philosophy and teachings of God-fearing men who received the respect of their fellowmen because of their age, knowledge, and experience. One of the distinctive elements of Job and other Wisdom Literature is the success syndrome that runs throughout the narrative. People of Old Testament times believed that a wise man not only achieved personal success but also could teach others how to succeed. Before Job's trials, he too had been numbered among the successful "wise men" of his day (1:1-3; 4:3). He later regained that status when God restored him.

Even more clearly than most other Wisdom Literature, Job illustrates the importance of asking the right questions, exploring the possible answers fully, and applying the answers to specific life situations. The writer of Job increased the teaching effectiveness of this technique by leaving the solution open-ended so that readers must reach their own conclusions. Furthermore, the author dealt with the type of timeless questions that still puzzle persons of today.

A significant, but frequently overlooked, theme in Job is the blessing-curse element. A thorough study of Job reveals many examples of this element. The most dominant blessing-curse themes occur in Job's *blessing* of prosperity (1:1-3); the *curse* of his loss of his children, possessions, and health (2:13 to 42:9); and the *blessing* of his return to prosperity (42:10-17). Other evidences of this theme appear somewhat less conspicuously throughout the book.

The writing of Job extended over a long period of time and involved more than one unknown author. Some scholars believe that its writing began as early as 1000 BC but did not conclude until sometime between 500 and 300 BC. Others believe it began no earlier than the seventh century BC. No one really knows who wrote the book. Conjectures as to the author or authors include Job, Elihu, Moses, Solomon, Heman, Isaiah, Hezekiah, and Baruch. Certain expressions in the book lead scholars to believe that the author originally wrote the book in Arabic and later translated it into Hebrew. However, the evidence still remains inconclusive. Egypt, Mesopotamia, Akkadia, Greece, and India have ancient literature with a parallel or similar plot.

Many readers of Job have a mistaken idea of the purpose and meaning of the book. A noted British theologian once pointed out that if the author of Job intended to solve the mystery of suffering, he failed glaringly. He reasoned that the writer proved neither that sin caused *all* suffering nor that it did not cause *any*. Other scholars disagree with the commonly-held view that the book deals with the proverbial "patience of Job." They argue that patience is only one of several themes in the book and that it really does not reflect the central teachings of the book. Readers must therefore deal with the question: What, then, is the purpose and meaning of Job?

The purpose of the book includes several elements. Job seeks to explore (not solve) the problem of suffering, especially as it relates to righteous persons. The book grapples with the questions of how or when sin relates to suffering and why a just God permits evil to exist. It provides encouragement for a nation that has suffered much throughout history. It illustrates God's permanence in contrast to the transience of earthly possessions. Most of all, however, Job conveys the message that people will never fully comprehend the mystery of suffering. The key seems to lie in trusting God to sustain righteous persons in suffering rather than in understanding why they must suffer.

Readers who accept this as the purpose of Job will better understand the meaning of the book. The book portrays both man's faith in God and God's faith in man. Basically, however, the book narrates a man's struggle with faith in the face of innocent suffering and unanswered questions. In that respect the man Job becomes the representative worshiper of every generation.

The Book of Job contains many forms of literature: drama, narrative, poetry, proverbs, laments, instruction, dialogue. One of the most popular ways of viewing it is as drama, since it lends itself so well to that form (a prologue, five scenes, and an epilogue). However, this commentary will treat Job as a debate. The debate involves an exploration of suffering—its meaning, causes, and cures—but mostly its effect on faith. Side issues in the debate relate to the problem of the prosperity of the wicked and an examination of the justice and power of God. In studying the book, the reader needs to remember, though, that the literary form only serves as a vehicle to carry the message. The form does not negate the historical existence of the man Job or the reality of his suffering and restoration.

In spite of its antiquity, Job remains a book for all times. Persons of today still wrestle with problems of faith, suffering, sin, discouragement, grief, and misunderstanding by their contemporaries. Modern readers can both empathize with and learn from Job's experiences in his pilgrimage of faith.

Job's Background and Situation
1:1 to 2:13

The Book of Job is a daring book. It challenges people to reexamine popular theology, explore the reasons for their personal suffering, and reconsider how to counsel others in painful circumstances. It suggests such questions as whether Job (and people of today) should view pain as divine punishment or as divine confidence in the faith of the sufferer. The book also dares to probe the problem of apparent injustices in life, such as why evil people often seem to prosper. It exposes the folly of blind or shallow answers to some of the harsh realities of life.

The problem of the suffering of righteous persons, as illustrated by Job, is a major theme in the book. Nevertheless, Job remains primarily a book about faith. It probes both the dark and bright sides of faith—the agonizing struggle and the inspiring triumph of trust and hope. It poses the kind of questions that many suffering persons would like to ask, but do not dare. Job, therefore, has an appeal for all persons who have wrestled with the problem of clinging to faith in the face of suffering.

Character and Status of Job (1:1-5)

The Book of Job begins with a concise statement that describes the geographical and spiritual background of the narrative. Job resided in a land identified only as "Uz." The exact location of Uz has been the subject of much debate. Commentators have variously located it as part of Edom, Arabia, or Syria, or as a land dominated by one of these nations. The writer described the man Job as blameless ("perfect"—KJV, meaning complete and well-rounded) and upright. Job "feared God," a characteristic of persons technically identified as "wise men." Job's God-fearing nature resulted in his turning away from evil (v. 1). The same four descriptions of Job (blameless, upright, feared God, and turned away from evil) appear in 1:1, 1:8, and 2:3.

Verses 2-3 support the claim that Job had a "blameless and upright character" by listing his possessions. Possessions, whether in the form of children or material wealth, indicated to the Oriental mind that the person's righteousness had put him in good stead with God. Conversely, Orientals viewed poverty, suffering, and lack of children as punishment for sin. The next verse implies that Job stood in good stead with God. Job had seven sons and three daughters, ideal by Hebraic standards both in number and proportion. In addition, Job had much livestock: seven thousand sheep, three thousand camels, five hundred yokes of oxen, and five hundred she-asses (v. 3). He also had many servants.

Job and his family lived in high style (1:4-5).—Each son lived in a separate house—uncommon in an era when even married sons generally brought their wives to their father's home with them to live. According to verse 4, these sons took turns entertaining their brothers and sisters with a feast. Meanwhile Job continued to guard their spiritual welfare. He offered burnt offerings in their behalf on a regular basis. The writer does not imply that Job thought his children deliberately sinned. Rather, he suggests that Job provided burnt offerings as a precautionary measure. Job may have feared that his sons might have sinned unintentionally (v. 5). Technically, a linguist could translate the word "cursed" in verse 5 as either *cursed* or *blessed*. If the word means *blessed*, rather than *cursed*, it could signify that Job sanctified his sons and offered sacrifices for them (a patriarchal duty) and that the sons then blessed God.

The point remains that Job lived a righteous life in spite of the temptations that come with prosperity. He also maintained a religious concern for his children. The Christian reader can appreciate Job's uprightness more fully in view of the statements about the perils of wealth to one's spiritual life outlined in the New Testament (Matt. 19:23; Luke 12:15-21; 1 Tim. 6:9; Jas. 5:3).

Job's Trials Begin (1:6-22)

The preceding verses have merely served as a setting for the book, informing the reader of Job's background and character. Verses 6-22 mark the beginning of Job's trials. The narrative of the suffering of this man of faith opens with an event that took place in heaven.

Decision to try Job's righteousness (1:6-12).—The heavenly council ("sons of God," v. 6) was an idea Israel shared with other neighboring countries. Israel believed that her God was the only real God, and he ruled over lesser beings who served him. (1 Kings 22:19-23 gives a very clear picture of this heavenly council.) Satan's identification as part of the heavenly council puzzles modern readers. Some interpreters understand the ancient idea about "the Satan" as being different from the later idea of Satan as a fallen angel. At this point Satan was the Adversary, a special accuser and/or prosecutor upon the earth—a sort of special spy.

Some interpreters understand the "day" (v. 6) the council met to be New Year's Day. According to ancient belief, on New Year's Day God wrote the names of righteous people in the book of life and blotted out those of wicked ones. Others do not see a special significance.

Verse 7 brings the reader to the actual conversations that took place at the council meeting. The Lord asked Satan where he had been, to which question Satan replied: "From going to and fro on the earth." Satan's answer suggests that he had been carrying out his appointed function of acting as a "spy from the sky."

The Lord perceived Satan's skepticism about humanity. He asked the question, "Have you considered my servant Job?" (v. 8). He then mentioned the four characteristics of Job listed in verse 1: blameless, upright, feared God, and turned away from evil. The fact that these four traits of Job appear in both of these verses, then again in 2:3, implies that Job's character had a strong bearing on the narrative.

Satan accepted the Lord's question as a challenge. He resolved to prove that if Job lost his possessions, Job would also soon lose his righteousness and would defy ("stop blessing") God. Verse 12 surfaces an important point: God trusted Job enough to allow him to be severely tested. This test, and the ones to follow, caused Job great suffering, but they also represented high honor. Even basically righteous persons will sometimes break, or at least falter, under the pressure of severe stress. God must have had great confidence in Job's character to allow Satan to put Job through such severe testing. By agreeing to let Satan administer the test, God left himself vulnerable to Job's possible failure. Suffering has already been mentioned as one important theme in the Book of Job. Another significant theme is the one discussed above: Job's trust in God and God's confidence in Job.

The first four tests (1:13-22).—The unsuspecting Job and his family were engaged in their normal routines of life when the first calamity came upon them. A messenger broke the bad news to Job that a group of marauding Arabs ("Sabeans" from modern Yemen) had stolen Job's cattle and asses and slain his servants. Only the messenger had escaped the massacre (v. 15). A review of verses 2-3 gives a grim reminder of the great loss Job sustained: five hundred yokes of oxen and five hundred she-asses.

Before the first messenger finished telling his grim story, a second messenger appeared on the scene. He told Job that a "fire of God" (probably lightning) had consumed Job's sheep and his servants. Again, the messenger alone had escaped.

The third test came when another messenger told Job that nomadic tribesmen (the Chaldeans) had formed three companies to surround and capture Job's three thousand valuable camels. This servant, too, was the sole survivor of the servants who had attended the camels.

While the third messenger still spoke, a fourth messenger came (v. 18). He brought the most devastating news of all. He said that while Job's children ate and drank in the home of one of the sons (a custom discussed in the commentary on v. 4), a violent wind had destroyed the home. As a result, all the young people had died. Since fathers viewed their sons as extensions of themselves, they felt that no greater calamity could come to a man than to have no son to carry on the family line. Verse 19 concludes with the same terse statement found in verses 15, 16, and 17: "I alone have escaped to tell you."

Job had remained seated during the time the other three messengers delivered their shocking messages. When he learned of the death of his children, however, he stood up (v. 20). Job then carried out the usual mourning rites: he tore his garments and shaved the hair from his head and beard. These acts signified that he had been stripped of his former status. Job "fell upon the ground" (a further sign of humility and submission).

Verse 21 deserves special attention. Job had lost virtually all his most precious possessions, including his own children. Nevertheless, instead of cursing God as Satan had predicted (v. 11), Job praised God. He confessed that the same God who had blessed his life had the right to remove those blessings. "In all this Job did not sin or charge God with wrong" (v. 22).

Job had passed the first four tests with inspiring faith and grace, but his trials had only begun. The question remained: How much suffering can even a righteous man endure and still remain faithful to God? The remaining chapters of the book reveal an increasing focus on this question.

His Trials Increase (2:1-13)

A person's state of health can greatly influence how he or she handles other kinds of stress. The next few verses reveal that Satan staked his reputation on the belief that loss of personal health would cause Job to surrender to the temptation to sin. Job had remained faithful to God during his trials in *good* health, but how would he react in *ill* health? This question led Satan to propose the next trial—a direct attack on Job's personal health.

The heavenly council meets again (2:1-6).—Chapter 2 begins by repeating the ritual already described in 1:6-8. The heavenly council, including Satan, stationed themselves before the Lord in an adversary position. During the conversation, the Lord reminded Satan that Job had remained faithful in spite of Satan's unjustifiable harassment of Job.

Satan responded with a proverb. He said, in essence, that a man will do anything necessary to save his own skin. Satan reasoned that

Job could cope with the loss of his property, servants, and even his own children more easily than with the loss of his personal health. (Note: Another interpretation of "skin for skin" in v. 4 involves the concept of bartering, such as the skin of his animals or children in exchange for his own skin.) Satan carried the challenge still a step further. He said that if the Lord would smite Job *below* the skin, Job would react by cursing God (v. 5).

The Lord's confidence in Job remained unshaken. God did not personally afflict Job as Satan had demanded, but he allowed Satan to do it. However, he added the condition that Satan must spare Job's life.

Job faces affliction (2:7-13).—Verse 7 implies immediacy in Satan's affliction of Job's body. The term "loathsome sores" (v. 7) scarcely conveys the torturous condition described later in the account. A scanning of Job 7:5,14; 19:17; 30:17,30; and 3:25 will give the reader a more complete understanding of the pain, disfigurement, and mental anguish involved in the disease. The descriptions of these "loathsome sores" have led to the possible diagnosis of leprosy, elephantiasis, an infestation of boils, or some other severe skin disease.

Verse 8 pictures Job sitting in the ashes scraping himself with a piece of a broken earthen vessel ("potsherd"). Interpreters have suggested two possible reasons for Job's use of the potsherd: (1) to scratch the skin to alleviate itching; and (2) to symbolize grief. The "ashes" described in verse 8 refer to the dunghill outside the city (equivalent to our city dumps). Only outcasts and mourners would inhabit these odoriferous dunghills.

Verses 9-12 contain three contrasting, possible responses to Job's plight: (1) Give up, (2) accept it graciously, and (3) weep about it. Notice how Job's wife, Job himself, and Job's friends initially responded.

(1) Job's wife advised him to "give up." She believed Job would be better off dead than alive in his current state. As in 1:5, the word translated "curse" (v. 9) poses a problem, since the same Hebrew word means both *bless* and *curse*. In both cases, however, the advice would lead to the same result. Job could either *curse* God and receive death as a consequence, or *bless* God, then give up and die.

(2) Job personally believed a sufferer should "accept it graciously."

He maintained that people must accept the bad with the good in life, since God had the right to send both good and evil. Job compared his wife's impetuous suggestion to the type one might expect from the group usually referred to as "foolish women." Note that Job did not call his wife a foolish woman. He merely said that she had spoken like one.

(3) Job's friends' initial reaction to Job's plight was to "weep about it." First, they wept at the sight of him when they saw his disfigured condition, then they went through the ritual of mourning for him for seven days and nights. The time element of "silent mourning" (vv. 12-13) suggests that they treated Job as though he were already dead. (Traditionally, friends devoted seven days and nights in mourning for the dead.)

Another insight relating to the friends appears here. Generally Hebrews ostracized people with Job's kind of ailment because they considered it ritually unclean. The willingness of Job's friends to break Hebrew tradition suggests that they were not Hebrews and thus not subject to Levitical laws about uncleanness. Eliphaz came from Teman (probably Edom); Bildad from Shuah (Edom or Arabia); and Zophar from the land of the Naamathites (northwest Arabia). These three friends appear in verses 11-13 as compassionate persons who came from long distances to comfort Job.

In summary, the prologue of Job (1:1 to 2:13) portrays Job as a righteous man who was trying to accept unjust suffering graciously. Likewise, it pictures Job's friends as counselors who sincerely hoped to help Job find a way out of his suffering. The prologue gives no hint of the heated debate to follow.

First Round of the Debate
3:1 to 14:22

Chapter 2 concluded by stating that when Job's shocked friends saw his plight, they sat in mournful silence with him for seven days and nights. Chapter 3 begins with the words "after this," denoting that the interval of silence had ended. Job himself took the initiative in speaking, thus beginning the first round of the debate to follow.

Job: First Round (3:1-26)

The words "opened his mouth" (v. 1) served as a literary device in the Bible to call attention to an important message to follow. The announcement with which Job broke the silence came with bombastic force. He pronounced a curse upon the day of his birth, saying, "Let the day perish wherein I was born,/and the night which said/'A man-child is conceived'" (v. 3). The blessing-curse theme, a prevalent theme throughout the book, appears here in reference to Job's birth. Generally the Hebrews received the news of conception and birth as a great blessing. In this case the blessing became a curse because of the circumstances that later plagued Job's life.

The first round of the debate, therefore, began with a death wish, the validity of which Job's friends could not let go unchallenged. Later chapters narrate their response to Job's outcry.

Verses 3-9 include another theme in Job—light and darkness. Job used this theme to support the blessing-curse theme in these verses. Light symbolized "good" (blessing) and darkness "evil" (curse). Verses 4-9 contain an interplay of the figures. The curse Job put on the day of his birth involved turning the day into darkness and the night into unlighted blackness. Job wished that he had never been born (v. 10).

"Why did I not die at birth?" (3:11-19).—In order to understand Job's reasoning in verses 11-19, the reader must remember the overwhelming losses Job had faced. Job had lived a righteous life, yet had been stripped of all his earthly blessings. He had no way of knowing that his disastrous state had resulted from a satanic plot, not from rejection by God. No wonder he became morbidly depressed.

Job reasoned that if his destiny was undeserved suffering, he would have been better off if he had not been born alive. He thought that if he had been born dead, he at least would have rested peacefully in a sort of nonexistent state. Job imagined himself sleeping in death with kings, wise men, and princes. The small and the great would have equality there. Death puts all on the same level (v. 19).

The irony of life (3:20-26).—Job moved from fanciful thinking to stark realism in verses 20-26. Here he reflected on the irony of life. The miserable person who longs for death does not receive it. The implication was that, in contrast, the happy person who wants to live dies.

Job viewed himself as a person "hedged in" (v. 23) by God. He expressed the thought that God had provided light for his path, but no way to find the light. These words probably alluded to the fact that Job's suffering so overshadowed his life that he could not see beyond it. His suffering and complaints came as regularly as his daily bread and water.

The concluding words of Job's speech in the first round of the debate summarize Job's plight. The worst possible straits that he could imagine had come to him. He could find no ease, peaceful quiet, or rest. The only thing that he could count on coming with regularity was trouble.

Eliphaz: First Round (4:1 to 5:27)

Job's friends had listened quietly while Job delivered his first speech. Although they had mourned Job's suffering, they evidently felt duty-bound to correct his theology. Eliphaz the Temanite, the eldest of the friends, spoke out first. Thus began the first response to Job's speech.

Eliphaz presses the charges (4:1-21).—People usually feel reluctant to kick somebody when he is down, and especially a friend. Sometimes, however, one must hurt a person in order to help him. Eliphaz probably assessed Job's situation in just that light. He believed his friend had erred and must be brought to repentance before God would restore him. As in Job's case, Job's friends had no way of knowing about Satan's plot. They naturally assumed that his suffering had come as punishment for sin.

Eliphaz began with an apology for adding to Job's misery, but he said that he could not remain silent (v. 2). He reminded Job of how many people Job had instructed and strengthened in the past. (The word *instructed*, v. 3, connotes correction.) Eliphaz said, in effect, that Job knew how to help others with their problems but could not deal with his own. As if to soften the blow, he added a note of confidence about Job's piety and conduct. However, he quickly moved away from any further mention of Job's virtues.

Having dispensed with the niceties, Eliphaz laid down the cold facts. He asked Job if he had ever heard of innocent people being punished by God. The implied answer was, "No; God only punishes evildoers." The reference to the lion in verses 10-11 has two possible meanings. (1) Lions sometimes symbolized evildoers, as in Psalm 17:12. (2) Lions roared when they lost their strength—and so had Job!

Eliphaz then shared a secret. He said that he had had a dream that left him trembling and caused his hair to stand on end. In the dream a figure stood before him and asked, "Can mortal man be righteous before God? Can a man be pure before his Maker?" (v. 17). Eliphaz asked how mere humans can claim sinlessness if even God's angels have sinned. He reminded Job that God can crush sinful mortals as easily as man crushes a moth, the most destructive but easiest to kill of all creatures. He added that man has no guarantee of living long enough to attain wisdom.

Eliphaz' discourse continued (5:1-27).—Eliphaz pursued still another possibility. He had not observed Job praying. Perhaps that fact led him to ask where Job sought intercession: to which "holy ones" (angels) had he turned for help? Eliphaz said that Job would receive no more intercession from angels than from the local center of justice ("gate," v. 4). Neither would offer him any help.

An important focus in chapter 5 and throughout each of the friends' discourses relates to the fact that people bring trouble on themselves through their sins. Based on this assumption, Eliphaz's counsel to Job was to rid himself of his troubles by seeking God's forgiveness and deliverance (v. 8). Eliphaz then reminded Job of God's power, wisdom, and compassion, concluding with a beatitude about the redemptive benefits of receiving God's punishment. The implication in verse 17, of course, was that Job's suffering had resulted from sin.

Again Eliphaz extolled God, this time by enumerating the troubles from which God promised to deliver his people (vv. 19-26). The numbers "six" and "seven" in verse 19, loosely translated, mean "more than a large number of times." Eliphaz had found these promises to be trustworthy. He advised Job to experience God's deliverance for himself.

Job's Response (6:1 to 7:21)

The proverbial "patience of Job" comes to a grinding halt in chapter 6. Job's response to the speech of Eliphaz dispels any false notions that the Book of Job relates to patience. As explained in the introduction to this commentary, the book is an attempt to explore the suffering of a righteous person. Chapters 6—7 deal with the "dark side of faith."

A heavy burden (6:1-30).—Just as Eliphaz could not let Job's statements go unchallenged, so Job could not remain silent about Eliphaz's charges. Job's reply portrays him as finally dealing openly with his anger and doubts—a stage in the grief process of most sufferers.

Job began with an overall statement of the weight of his grief (v. 2). In verse 5, he said, in effect: Why *shouldn't* I cry out against this undeserved suffering? It is as natural as the ass braying and the ox lowing. Job viewed Eliphaz's criticism as tasteless and repulsive (vv. 6-7). Another possible interpretation of these verses is that Job's existence had become loathsome.

Consider the basis of Job's anguished complaints. (1) He believed that God had treated him as an enemy, sending poisoned darts of suffering into his life—verse 4. (2) He had nothing to live for, yet God made him live on—verses 8-13. (3) His friends had failed him—verses 14-20. (4) He had made no demands on his "comforters," but they had been too repelled by his appearance to comfort him—verses 21-23.

Up to this point Job had heard nothing but bold generalities and vague insinuations from Eliphaz. Job therefore invited him to give a concrete example of Job's wrongdoing that could have brought this suffering on him.

In verses 26-30 Job turned the tables on his friends by becoming the critic instead of the one criticized. He accused Eliphaz of regarding Job's words of anguish as mere wind. (Today persons might call it "hot air.") Job angrily accused his friend of being willing to cast lots over the fatherless for the purpose of enslaving them or bartering to possess a friend (v. 27).

Job concluded this segment by asking Eliphaz to look at him and see if he looked like a liar. Job maintained that he could still distinguish calamity when it came.

A hopeless existence (7:1-21).—Chapter 7 records a continuation of Job's response to the first speech of Eliphaz. Here, however, instead of directing the words to Eliphaz, he directed them to God. Job compared man's existence on earth to that of a slave or forced laborer. He complained of being tired but unable to sleep; of having his flesh covered with worms and dust; of having a life as transient as a cloud. The word translated *hope* in verse 6 also means "thread." Here Job used it as a pun. He said that he had run out of *hope*, like a weaver runs out of *thread*.

Job's hopeless state manifested itself in his complaints to God about the way God had treated him. First, Job asked if he were a primeval sea or sea monster that God had to guard in order to maintain security (v. 12). Job then complained that when he tried to sleep during his illness, God scared him with nightmares. Job asked why God bothered to magnify man if God intended to test him every moment (v. 18). Compare this verse with Psalm 8:4.

Job climaxed his complaint to God by referring to God as a man-watcher and asking what he had ever done to God to make him God's target (v. 20). In conclusion he asked why God did not show his divine forgiveness while Job still lived. Job anticipated that he would soon die, and it would be too late then.

Bildad: First Round (8:1-22)

A second friend, Bildad, enters the debate in chapter 8. Verse 1 identifies Bildad as a Shuhite (locale uncertain, but possibly Edom or Arabia).

Bildad did not preface his first speech with a respectful comment, as Eliphaz had done. He immediately launched into an expression of righteous indignation at Job's theological stance. In effect, Bildad told Job to "shut up" and listen (v. 2). He asked, rhetorically, if God perverts justice. Bildad then added that if Job prayed to God and became pure and upright, he would receive God's reward.

Bildad advised Job to look to past history and learn from it. He reminded Job that those who forgot God always perished, just as papyrus and reeds perish when deprived of water (vv. 11,13). The ungodly person could depend on nothing to support him. Bildad made his point with the imagery of seeking support from a spider's web, a falling house, and a plant rooted around stones.

The speech ended with Bildad's expression of trust that God will not reject an upright person any more than he will help an evil one. Verses 21-22 imply that Bildad still hoped for Job's restoration.

Job's Response (9:1 to 10:22)

The Book of Job uses an interesting literary technique. The speaker in the narrative did not necessarily respond to the person who had immediately preceded him in speaking. Chapters 9 and 10 illustrate that technique. Job did not answer Bildad (whose speech immediately preceded Job's), but rather he responded to Eliphaz who had spoken earlier. By that time perhaps Job had found time to formulate a more effective argument against what Eliphaz had said.

Job's need for an umpire (9:1-35).—Job's opening words in chapter 9 apparently relate to the dream of Eliphaz (4:17). A "spirit" had asked Eliphaz if mortals could appear righteous in God's eyes. Job agreed with the negative answer implied by the spirit. In fact, his whole speech in chapter 9 focused on man's inability to appeal to God for justification. Job said that he needed an umpire to settle the matter between God and himself (v. 33).

The source of tension was God's omnipotence versus man's weakness. Job asked how man could hope to argue against a God who could move mountains, cause earthquakes, stretch out the heavens, and do numerous other great deeds. Job said that he could not even *see* God when God passed by! How, then, could he hope to argue with God? He reasoned that in spite of his innocence, he could not plead his case effectively. In this questioning time of his suffering, Job imagined God to be an unjust ruler who destroyed the righteous along with the wicked (vv. 5-22). Job even blamed God for unjust earthly judges (v. 24).

Verses 25-30 reflect Job's innermost fears. He assumed that he would die soon and that God would judge him guilty. No amount of cleansing would save him from God's wrath. He thought he had a hopeless case.

Job figured that if God were a man, he could go to court with him and have a fair trial—but God was not a man. Job wished that an umpire would come and mediate impartially (v. 33). Then Job could speak without being afraid.

Job's despair (10:1-22).—Job reacted to intense suffering like many persons of today do. He lashed out against God while trying to come to terms with his suffering. Most persons eventually work through this stage and see life in a different perspective. So did Job, but not at this point in the narrative.

Chapter 10 contains both an outpouring of Job's grief and a lashing out at God. Job accused God of despising the human creature he had made and of being unable to empathize with the plight of mortals. He pictured God as molding man, then destroying him. The words "cheese . . . flesh . . . bones and sinews" (vv. 10-11) refer to the conception and growth of the fetus, a miracle made possible by God. Job said that God gave him life and love, knowing all the time that he would make Job suffer.

Next Job accused God of trying to catch him in a sin (v. 14). Job felt like a hunted animal whom God continued to attack. In despair Job asked why God had let him be born. He closed this speech by requesting that God leave him alone so that he could find a little comfort before he died (vv. 20-22).

Zophar: First Round (11:1-20)

Job's third friend, Zophar, had remained silent until then. He was probably the youngest of the three men and had waited to speak until the others had expressed themselves. When Zophar spoke, however, he displayed no timidity.

Zophar began by asking if nobody would rebuke Job's idle and mocking words (vv. 2-3). Job's assertion that his doctrine was pure had especially aroused Zophar's ire. Zophar wished that God would speak out against Job, but since God did not, Zophar would do it for him.

Actually, Zophar felt that God gave Job far less punishment than Job deserved. He sarcastically asked if Job thought he could comprehend the greatness of God (height, depth, length, and breadth, vv. 8-9). He agreed with Job on one fact, though: nobody could hinder God. However, Zophar applied it to mean that when God saw evil, he recognized it and punished it.

Verses 13-19 indicate that Zophar had not completely given up hope about Job in spite of his earlier statements. He appealed to Job to repent of his sins and seek God's forgiveness. Under these conditions Job would stop suffering. Zophar concluded with the warning in verse 20 that the unrepentant will not escape. Their only hope will be death.

Job's Final Response in the First Round (12:1 to 14:22)

Job 12:1 to 14:22 contains a long summation of Job's argument about his suffering. This speech concludes the first round of the debate. Job addressed the first portion to all of the friends, not just to Zophar. He addressed the second portion to God.

Job understands God's power (12:1-25).—Job began his last

speech of the first round on a sarcastic note: "No doubt . . ./wisdom will die with you" (v. 2). His friends thought that they had a corner on wisdom, but Job, too, had a mind. Nobody had to tell *him* about God's power!

At that point in his suffering Job felt that the lessons he had learned about God's power had only negative value. He said that God had allowed him, a righteous person, to become a source of ridicule; had permitted robbers' households to prosper; and had given security to those who made a god of their own power (v. 6). These lessons had not lowered Job's estimate of God's power. They had reinforced it. Job knew what all of nature knew—that God had his powerful hand in everything that happened (vv. 7-12).

Verses 13-24 confirm the latter statement. Job credited God with wisdom, might, counsel, and understanding. He said that nobody could rebuild what God tore down or release what God imprisoned. God could cause droughts or floods, control the deceived and the deceiver, strip the power from counselors, and make fools of judges. Neither kings, priests, elders, or princes were immune to God's power. Even the darkness of Sheol could not shrink from God's reach (v. 22). Job added that God could even cause chiefs (leaders) to become like drunkards, groping to find their way in the darkness (v. 25).

Fake healers and a vengeful God (13:1-28).—Job said to his friends that they knew what he had said was true, so they should let him argue his case with God (vv. 1-3).

Before pleading his case with God, however, Job had some more words to say to his friends. He accused them of whitewashing with lies and of being quack doctors ("worthless physicians"). He wished that they would just exercise wisdom by remaining silent. Job reproved his friends for trying to ingratiate themselves with God by defending him against Job's charges. He called their pious platitudes "proverbs of ashes" (v. 12).

Having vented his anger against his friends, Job took his life in his hand by directing his accusations toward God (v. 14). He knew that God could slay him for what he was about to say. Job's only hope lay in the belief that he would be able to come into God's presence when he died, something a wicked person could not do. Therein would lie Job's vindication (v. 18).

Verses 20-28 contain a record of Job's dangerous challenge to God. He began with the petition that God stop intimidating him (v. 21) and that God specify the alleged sins that had resulted in Job's suffering (v. 23). After receiving no answer, Job pressed another question. Why had God treated him like an enemy? What sport was there in frightening a "driven leaf" (v. 25—a reference to Job's helpless state). He accused God of treating him like a slave or prisoner and letting him waste away like a rotten or moth-eaten object.

The lot of a human (14:1-22).—Chapter 14 contains a familiar commentary on the status and limitations of human beings upon this earth. Job complained that a person's life is brief and full of trouble. He asked why God even bothered with such a vulnerable creature (v. 3). He suggested that since man had such a short life, God should leave him alone and let him enjoy the time he had.

Job commented that a tree has hope because even if someone cuts it down, it can sprout again. When a man dies, however, he cannot rise again (vv. 7-12). Job's anguish led him to say that even if he had to wait in Sheol till God got over being angry, he would gladly do it for the sake of speaking with God.

Some interpreters see in verse 14 a visionary hope for an afterlife. Others feel that the context of the verse supports instead Job's wish to have God listen in a just manner to Job's side of the story. After God heard Job's story, he would judge Job fairly and would again love and protect Job. Furthermore, God would then seal up Job's sins in a bag where they could never be seen (vv. 15-17).

The first round of the debate ends here. The experience of Job parallels that of many persons of today as they try to cope with their own suffering. Some present-day sufferers are still working through the "blaming God" stage of their pain. Others are guilt-ridden over imagined sins that they think caused them to be punished through pain. Both need to keep struggling until they work through these dark times of despair and doubt and are at peace with God and self.

Whether Job had a vision of the afterlife or not, Christians do. Christians have the promise that no matter what happens in this life, they have the assurance of a joyous, pain free life to come. This promise puts suffering in proper perspective: a painful, but not hopeless experience.

Second Round of the Debate
15:1 to 21:34

The second round of the debate begins with a speech by Eliphaz. The reader will note a difference in direction taken here. Although the first round contained many barbed statements, it had a redemptive purpose. All three friends hoped that their verbal chastisement would bring Job to his senses and make him repent. In the second round, however, the focus turns from redemption to destruction. The friends change from "constructive criticizers" to "judgmental jurors" determined to find Job guilty of the alleged sins that caused his suffering.

Eliphaz: Second Round (15:1-35)

Earlier in the debate Eliphaz had described Job as one who had instructed and strengthened others in a counseling capacity (4:3-4). He was a "wise man" by ancient technical standards. In verses 2-4, Eliphaz stated that if Job were really wise, he would not be delivering "hot air." The east wind, known as "sirocco," was a violent wind. Eliphaz meant, therefore, that Job had spoken in a violent and irreverent way, rather than in the pious way expected of a wise man.

Eliphaz charged that Job had actually condemned himself by what he had said (vv. 5-6). Eliphaz implied that Job's questioning of God's motives proved that he deserved the punishment he received.

What made Job think he was superior? *(15:7-16).*—Eliphaz pressed his charges against Job in biting words. He asked if Job were the first man on earth and thus had either the privilege of eavesdropping on the divine council or had special claim to its wisdom. Eliphaz called attention to his equality with Job. (People of ancient times credited the elders with superior wisdom.) Eliphaz implied that because of his age, he too had a claim to wisdom.

The "consolations of God" of which Eliphaz spoke in verse 11 are somewhat puzzling. Thus far the narrative has contained no account of God's comforting Job in any way. The reader can only assume that Eliphaz referred to the backhanded comfort extended to him by the friends who considered themselves agents of God. (In 16:2 Job called his friends "miserable comforters.")

Eliphaz accused Job of arrogance and rebellion against God because of what Job had said. Verse 14 reiterates the thought of 4:17 that nobody can really appear righteous in God's eyes. Verse 15 repeats the statement Eliphaz had made in 4:18 concerning God's distrust, even of angels. Eliphaz rationalized that if God distrusted angels, he would distrust much more an abominable sinner like Job.

Eliphaz' homily on the cost of sin (15:17-35).—Eliphaz summoned Job to heed what Eliphaz had learned about wickedness. The words to follow may have been a rebuttal to Job's statement about God's injustice in letting robbers prosper.

First, Eliphaz spoke of how sin affects the conscience of the sinner. He maintained that a wicked person suffers more than appears on the surface. He "writhes in pain all his days" (v. 20), becomes paranoid (v. 21*a*), and dies (v. 21*b*). Furthermore, he cannot escape misfortune, unsuccessfully looks for bread, and fears the distress and anguish that attack him (vv. 22-24).

Verses 25-35 list the reasons Eliphaz gave for the suffering of an evil person. Primarily Eliphaz charged that suffering resulted from defying God. He asserted that a wicked person assaulted God by running against God as a stubborn warrior might do (v. 26). His wealth will not endure because of his lack of spiritual perception. If he trusts in empty riches, he will receive emptiness as his reward. Eliphaz summed up the matter by saying that the lot of all ungodly people is a barren existence. Verse 35 brings to mind Psalm 7:14: "Behold, the wicked man conceives evil,/and is pregnant with mischief,/and brings forth lies."

The implication of Eliphaz' homily is clear, though unjust. He inferred that Job's suffering resulted from hardened sin.

Job: Second Round (16:1 to 17:16)

Thus far Job's friends had offered nothing but pious platitudes, accusations, and self-righteous advice. They had shown little sensitivity to Job's needs in his time of depression. The most generous comment one can make in their defense is that they spoke in keeping with the accepted theology of their own day.

Job's rebuke of his friends (16:1-5).—In the second round of the debate Job aptly addressed his friends as "miserable comforters." Their kind of comfort only made Job's wounds worse. Job informed them that if the roles were reversed, he, too, could let pious platitudes roll off his tongue and shake his head disapprovingly. Job may have spoken the words of verse 5 sarcastically, or he may have meant that if the roles were reversed, he would act as a true comforter should.

Job's lament (16:6-17).—Job moved from censuring his friends to the more pressing matter of his own suffering. Nothing seemed to help his pain. Talking about his pain did not help, but *not* talking about it did not help either (v. 6).

Job concluded that the only explanation for his suffering was that God hated him. Job said that God's constant affliction had worn him out and left him with no friends to defend him (v. 7). He thought God had caused him to shrivel up (a probable reference to his lost weight), which in turn made Job appear even more guilty. Job accused God of tearing him angrily, of treating him with hostility, and of gnashing his teeth at him. Job blamed God for allowing evil men to treat him insolently (vv. 10-11).

Verses 12-17 contain the description of a completely broken man who believed that God had made him a target. Job thought that under God's command he had been torn asunder. He used forceful imagery to describe his plight: seized by the neck and dashed to pieces; surrounded by attackers; and vital organs slashed open and poured out (vv. 12-13). Job felt like a strong city whose walls of defense had been breached. In verse 15 the word "sackcloth" denotes mourning, and the words "laid my strength in the dust" relate to humiliation. Job described his face as "red with weeping" (v. 16). Some interpreters believe that the statement "on my eyelids is deep darkness" refers to dark circles around Job's eyes because of his illness. Verse 17 indicates that Job still defended his innocence.

An ironic plight (16:18 to 17:2).—The next few verses portray Job in the ironic position of expecting God, whom he thought was his attacker, to become his final defender.

Job pled that when he died his blood would remain uncovered on the ground (v. 18). The Hebrews believed that shed blood on the ground would cry out in behalf of the victim. God would hear the cry and avenge the death. (The account of Cain and Abel in Gen. 4:10 illustrates this belief.) However, verses 19-22 appear to refer to an "umpire" (as in 9:33) or an intercessor who will cause God to avenge Job's death. Job thought that his remaining time was brief.

He would soon be at a point of "no return." He wanted his innocence established before he died (v. 22).

Job 17:1-2 portrays Job as a broken man who could only look forward to the grave. Still unconvinced of Job's innocence, his friends continued to treat him in a hostile manner. He had no hope except that God might finally recognize his innocence and deliver him.

Appeal for help (17:3-16).—Using the legal terminology of that day, Job appealed to God to put down a "pledge" (bail) in Job's behalf until his case was resolved. He knew that nobody else would take his side (v. 3). He believed that God had afflicted him, but he still thought God would treat him more justly than his friends had. Verse 5 could either be a reminder to Job's friends, or it could be a side comment to God. The verse apparently means that the children of persons who betray a friend for profit will receive the curse of blindness.

Job's most consuming thoughts, however, related to the humiliation and suffering he had already endured. He had become a symbol of sin to those around them (a reference to the belief that suffering results from sin). People spat on him. Not only Job's eyes, but his whole body, revealed how this suffering had affected him physically (v. 7).

Interpreters have differing views of the meaning of verses 8-9. Some interpreters believe that the verses refer to a future time when righteous people will marvel at what happened to Job. Others think that the term "upright" applies to Job's self-righteous friends. Verse 10 contains an invitation to Job's friends to return to the debate. Job speculated that if they did, he would not find a "wise man" among them.

Job complained that death would soon come, leaving his purposes and plans unfulfilled. He asked, in effect: What hope is there, if my home is in Sheol? (vv. 13-16).

Bildad: Second Round (18:1-21)

By ancient standards all three of Job's friends bore the title of "wise men" (successful, intelligent men who knew how to apply their knowledge to life). Job's accusation that he could not find a wise man among them (17:10) therefore had struck a sensitive note.

Bildad had no intention of merely letting the matter drop. His response to Job's words revealed his defensiveness.

Bildad's rebuttal (18:1-4).—Bildad began his rebuttal by suggesting that Job had run out of arguments. He advised Job to think through the matter before the debate continued. The Hebrew word translated "you" (v. 2) is plural. Bildad may have meant "you and others sinners," thus identifying Job as a representative of the whole class of wicked people.

Verses 3-4 cut through to the reason for Bildad's defensiveness. In essence, Bildad said: "Look who has called *us* stupid! You, not your friends, expect God to change the order of the universe just for your benefit. You call us stupid, but you are the one who acted stupidly."

The destiny of the wicked (18:5-21).—According to ancient thought, a wicked person could only expect failure during his life. Bildad did not say directly that Job fell into that category, but he left that implication. Again, the reader needs to remember that Bildad had no way of knowing either the real reason for Job's suffering or that God would eventually vindicate Job. He could only assume that wickedness had caused this catastrophe in Job's life.

Bildad's description of the fate of the wicked began with the words "the light of the wicked is put out" (v. 5). A burning light in the family tent signified prosperity and success; darkness represented failure and disfavor in God's eyes. Bildad next described the feebleness that comes upon an evil person. He said that the stride of a wicked man shortens, he walks into traps, and terror follows close at his heels (vv. 7-11). Furthermore, the wicked man suffers from hunger, disease eats away his skin, and his confidence fails (vv. 12-14). Death ("king of terrors") comes to him. Strangers will dwell in his tent; nobody will remember him when he dies; he will have no family line (vv. 15-19). People everywhere will be horrified at the terrible death the wicked man must endure (v. 20).

Bildad concluded with the assertion that this was what an ungodly man could expect (v. 21). Most of the descriptions seemed to fit Job's plight exactly. Bildad likely reasoned that if Job had these problems, he had them because of his wickedness.

Job's Response (19:1-29)

Bildad's speech may have prompted Job's response in chapter 19, but Job addressed his words to *all* of the friends. Regardless of how well meaning the friends were, they had no insight into the real reason for Job's suffering. Their counsel, therefore, came across as self-righteousness, devoid of compassion for Job. However, since Job had no inkling of the real cause of his suffering either, he could only protest his innocence.

Having pointed out how his friends had wronged him, Job enlarged on how God had wronged him. God had not responded to Job's cry for help. Instead he had put barriers in Job's way and had even stripped Job of his previous honor (vv. 7-9). God had broken him down, pulling up his hope as one might uproot a tree (v. 10). Likely the most devastating act of all was the one described in verses 11-12: God had treated Job like an evil enemy.

The effect on family and friends (19:13-22).—Job was sensitive about the way his pitiful condition had affected other persons. He charged that God's affliction of him had estranged him from other members of the covenant community (v. 13). Even worse, the members of his own household forsook him. His wife and brothers considered him repulsive. Young children treated him with disrespect. All those whom he had loved had turned against him.

The gruesome description of verse 20 makes it understandable why his household and friends would turn away from him. He was as gaunt as a skeleton. The words "skin of my teeth" could either mean that his gums had receded so badly that his teeth barely hung to them, or that his teeth had eroded to the gums.

In spite of what "miserable comforters" his friends had been, Job implored them to pity him. He wanted them to recognize that his plight had resulted from God's hands, not his sin (v. 21). Job asked why his friends persecuted him like God did. What would it take to satisfy them? (v. 22).

Job's hope for eventual redemption (19:23-29).—Job expected his death to come soon. He feared that the truth about his innocence would remain unknown. He longed to write his defense in a book or better yet, engrave it on an imperishable rock (vv. 23-24).

Verse 25 contains the most frequently quoted words from the Book of Job: "I know that my Redeemer lives." The word *know* involves experiential knowledge, not mere intellect. The word *redeemer* referred to a kinsman who would vindicate a wrong done to his relative or who would "redeem" him from slavery, prison, or other oppression by paying for his release. Job expressed the confidence that his "Redeemer" still lived and would vindicate him.

Some interpreters see in verse 25 an early prophecy of the hope of resurrection that found ultimate fulfillment in Christ. Others see in it Job's personal hope that at the last minute God or his messenger would save him from death. Still others think Job still hoped that a kinsman would come to redeem him before he died. (The fact that the word *Redeemer* is capitalized in English translations does not necessarily prove that it refers to God, since Hebrew, the language of the Old Testament, has no capital letters. However, neither does it disprove it.)

Christians may differ in their understanding of verse 25, but they would agree on one fact. Christ became a redeemer of persons to a point that far exceeded Job's hope of redemption. Christ's redemptive sacrifice and his victory over death made possible the assurance for believers that they too will experience the resurrection. They will live because their Redeemer lives.

Verse 26 also poses difficult problems in translation and interpretation. The KJV says "in my flesh" and the RSV "from my flesh." Did Job mean that he would see God before he died or afterwards? Or, could he have meant that finally he would "see" the day when God would again be reconciled to him? Job added that he would see God and not a stranger ("not another," v. 27). Again, questions arise concerning the interpretation. Did Job mean that he, and not strangers, would see God, or that God would not be estranged from him? The meaning is unclear.

Job concluded this speech with a warning to his friends. If they continued to persecute him and to condemn him falsely, they would face God's wrath. Apparently Job maintained that after God heard Job's defense, he would take Job's side and vindicate him against his persecutors. In spite of Job's dark doubts because of his suffering, he still believed in divine justice (v. 29).

Zophar: Second Round (20:1-29)

Zophar's speech in the second round has a marked similarity to Bildad's. Both men had the same theme to which they tenaciously clung: the fate of wicked people. Zophar supported Bildad's speech but added no original thought. His speech comes across to the reader as little more than a "rubber stamp" on what Bildad said.

Reaction to Job's criticism (20:1-3).—Job's censure of his friends had stung Zophar. Like Bildad, Zophar became very defensive. He hastened to respond to Job's criticism. Job had insulted Zophar, and Zophar felt compelled to point out the truth to Job.

Zophar's tirade against the wicked (20:4-29).—Zophar at least began with a concession. He did not deny that wicked people enjoy temporary success (v. 5). However, he asserted that no matter how much prosperity an ungodly man seemed to gain, he would eventually perish shamefully and disappear from sight. His children would end up like poor beggars; they would have to make restitution for their father's wrongdoing. Zophar added that the wicked man might seem full of vigor for awhile, but he would die prematurely (v. 11).

In verses 12-14 Zophar compared wickedness to a sweet-tasting morsel that a wicked man allows to melt slowly under his tongue. As soon as the morsel melts, it turns into poison and causes the man to vomit. Zophar said that a wicked man swallows down riches but loses them like he loses the sweet morsel that turned to poison. Zophar continued his tirade in verses 16-29. He insisted that death (symbolized by the asp, v. 16) would come to the wicked man. This kind of person would not have the joy of looking upon rivers or using the fruit of his labor, for he had oppressed and robbed the poor. Due to his greed, the wicked man would not retain his wealth (vv. 20-21). God's wrath would descend on him like rain. The heavens and earth would witness against him. His possessions would be carried away.

The reader can almost picture Zophar pausing at that point to see if his words had attained the desired effect. Zophar did not call Job's name, but he left a clear implication that Job had better change his ways or the terrible things mentioned earlier would happen to *him* (v. 29).

Job's Final Response in Second Round (21:1-34)

Both Bildad and Zophar had built their case on the premise that wicked people can expect severe suffering during most of their lifetime and disgrace at their death. They avowed that any prosperity experienced by the wicked was quite limited in scope (20:5). Chapter 21 contains Job's response to the case they had built. Job maintained that they had built their entire case on a false assumption, and therefore their counsel had no value whatsoever.

An interesting feature of chapter 21 relates to Job's change in focus. Previously Job had mainly emphasized the suffering he had endured in spite of his *righteousness*. Here he stressed the prosperity that wicked men receive in spite of their *wickedness*.

A right to complain (21:1-6).—Job had already referred to his friends as "miserable comforters." He longed for real comfort and affirmation. He asked them at least to hear him out before they continued their mocking of him (vv. 2-3). Job reminded them rhetorically, however, that he had complained against God, not against them or other persons.

Job felt justified in complaining about his terrible plight and in becoming impatient. All his friends had to do was look at him if they wanted to see the appalling nature of his suffering. Laying of the hand upon the mouth (v. 5) signified awe and shock—the reaction of his friends when they looked upon him. Job shuddered to think of his own pitiful condition.

Rebuttal against the fate of the wicked (21:7-34).—People in Job's day, as now, tended to oversimplify the solution to problems and to deal in platitudes. Whether the oversimplification resulted from not knowing what else to say or from some other cause, it did not help Job much.

Job completely contradicted Zophar's platitude about the fate of the wicked. Zophar had said that wicked persons die young (v. 11); Job declared that they reach old age and remain powerful (v. 7). Zophar had stated that their children faced shame and poverty (v. 10); Job said that they remained secure, unchastened by God, and happy (vv. 8-9,11-13). Furthermore, all these blessings came to the wicked in spite of the fact that they had rejected God and had seen no profit in serving him. Job, on the other hand, had lived righteously, yet had suffered instead of prospered (v. 16).

Next, Job confronted another friend, Bildad, with the untrue truisms that Bildad had recited. Bildad had said that the burning light in the tent of the wicked would go out (symbol of failure, 18:5); Job challenged the truth of the statement (v. 17). Regarding the assertion that the children of wicked men receive punishment for their father's sins, Job insisted that a wicked person should have to pay for his own sins. His children should not have to suffer (vv. 19-21).

Interpreters differ in their understanding of verse 22. Possibly it relates to the fact that the friends acted as though they knew more than God. They knew that evil should be punished and righteousness rewarded. The problem was that God did not appear to share this view.

Verses 23-26 reveal the depression and hopelessness Job felt at that point. He had concluded that neither righteousness nor wickedness had any real bearing on a person's fate. For no apparent reason one person would enjoy contentment and good health all his life while another person would never even taste happiness. At death, decay and worms would eat away at the body of both the righteous and the wicked.

Job knew what his friends thought. They reasoned that if Job had lived righteously, he would live in luxury now instead of in his current deplorable condition. He insisted that they had based their rationale on misinformation both in regard to him and in their understanding of life. All who had lived awhile ("travel the roads," v. 29) could tell Job's friends that the wicked survive in the day of calamity and that nobody reproaches the wicked for his evil deeds.

Verse 34 sums up Job's rebuttal. The platitudes of his friends contained nothing but empty, meaningless phrases. They had built their whole case on false premises.

The second round of the debate does not reveal the whole story, but it does confront both Jewish and Christian readers of today with some important truths. (1) Oversimplifying the answers to life's problems is as unhelpful as overstating them. Friends usually neither expect nor want "pat answers" for every problem, but they do need affirmative love. (2) Persons in our generation are still tempted to jump to conclusions before all the facts are in. The wisest course is to minister to the sufferer and leave judgment about the cause of the suffering to God. (3) People still need to explore the possibility that they have built their case on false premises. Job's friends erred in thinking that all suffering resulted from sin. However, so did Job when he concluded that one's conduct has no effect on the amount of blessing one receives. Persons should avoid basing their opinions on broad generalizations. Not all persons bring suffering on themselves because of misconduct or abuse of their bodies. On the other hand, some of them do.

Third Round of the Debate
22:1 to 31:40

The third round of the debate between Job and his friends opens with a speech by Eliphaz. Previously Eliphaz had spoken mainly in generalities. He had suggested categories of sin in which Job might be guilty. In the third round, however, Eliphaz got down to specifics. Job's stubborn refusal to admit guilt may have prompted Eliphaz to intensify his attack. Whatever the case, Eliphaz spoke with great fervor.

Eliphaz: Third Round (22:1-30)

Eliphaz opened his argument by reminding Job that God had nothing to gain or lose by what happened to Job. Eliphaz probably intended this reminder to prove that God had no ulterior motive. Actually, however, verse 3 comes across as a parallel to what Job had said in 7:20, even though Eliphaz intended it to support something different.

Direct attack (22:4-11).—Some of the previous statements had been mere broad observations about sin. Verses 4-11, however, contain a direct attack on Job. Eliphaz sarcastically asked if Job thought that God had punished him for being *righteous*. (The irony was that in fact God had allowed Job to be tested through suffering because God did trust Job's righteousness.) Eliphaz concluded that since God punishes sin, not righteousness, God considered Job a sinner.

The charges made by Eliphaz had no basis in truth. Since Eliphaz had known Job for a long time and not observed his wickedness before, he thought Job must have been a "secret sinner." Eliphaz accused Job of treating the needy unjustly (v. 6), refusing water and food to the thirsty and hungry (v. 7), and showing partiality toward the powerful (v. 8). To these charges he added those of refusing to help widows and orphans (v. 9)—a particularly deplorable sin for a Hebrew to commit.

In verses 10-11 Eliphaz said, in effect: No wonder terror overwhelms you and death (darkness and floods) confront you! His implication was that a person should expect that kind of disaster if he behaved like Job.

God's transcendence (22:12-20).—Persons can view God's transcendence from very different perspectives. For example, righteous persons sometimes picture God as carefully and lovingly watching over them from an exalted position in the heavens. Evil persons, on the other hand, may think that because God is high above them, he cannot see them when they sin. In verses 12-30 Eliphaz accused Job of having the latter view. In reality, however, Job had described God as a "watcher of men" (7:20) who knew full well what transpired on earth below.

In ancient times people believed that God lived in the sky and that he used a cloud cover to separate his holiness from the sin of human beings. Eliphaz drew on this thought pattern when he accused Job of thinking that the cloud cover prevented God from seeing Job's sinful deeds (vv. 13-14).

Eliphaz' accusation was untrue, but he continued with the argument. He asked if Job intended to follow the example of evil people who had thought, "What can the Almighty do to us?" (v. 17). Eliphaz had already discussed the destruction that came to that kind of person—great floods that washed them away (v. 16).

Eliphaz reminded Job that righteous people delight in seeing the wicked punished (vv. 19-20). Regardless of how crude this attitude may sound to readers of today, it was an acceptable response in Job's day. Punishment of the wicked proved that God's system of justice still worked.

Call to repentance (22:21-30).—Eliphaz firmly believed that the only solution to Job's problem lay in repentance. Job must "Agree with God, and be at peace" (v. 21). Submission to God involved several conditions that Eliphaz outlined in verses 23-30. They included: a return to God, humbling of self, removal of sin from Job's life, putting confidence in God instead of in wealth. Eliphaz said that if Job followed these instructions, he would again receive answers to his prayers.

Verse 30 is not clear in the original language. It may mean that God will deliver innocent persons and that deliverance comes through clean hands (good works). In other words, you *are* what you *do.* If so, Eliphaz erred on two counts: (1) Job had not lived an evil life but rather a righteous one; and (2) even a righteous person must depend on God's grace, not good works, to deliver him.

Job: Third Round (23:1 to 24:25)

Job's reply in chapter 23 appears to be more introspective than argumentative. Job was trying to work through the very basic problem of how he could get God to listen to him. Before he could gain God's attention, however, he had to find God's hiding place. Chapter 23 focuses on Job's frustration in this search.

Although attributed to Job, chapter 24 completely breaks the line of thought of the previous chapter. Some interpreters believe that in the gathering process an editor inserted the chapter in the wrong order. Assuming that chapter 24 belongs in this order, however, Job's remarks moved from personal meditations in chapter 23 to general observations in chapter 24.

Job longs for access to God (23:1-17).—Job had cried out his complaints bitterly, but God continued to bring suffering upon him. Although he could feel God's hand heavy upon him, he could not find God in order to plead with him (v. 3). The word *find* relates to the hiddenness of God—an important biblical concept. From a positive viewpoint, God's hiddenness either refers to his transcendence or his waiting to reveal himself at the appropriate time, such as in the messianic role. In verse 3, however, Job viewed God's hiddenness from a negative standpoint. Job thought God had made himself inaccessible to suffering people. Earlier Job had wanted to be hidden from God, but in verse 3 he complained because God had hidden himself from Job.

The figure of Job laying his case before God in 23:4-7 suggests a court trial. Job speculated that if he could plead his case before God, as in a courtroom situation, God might listen to him and then explain the reason for his suffering. Job felt confident that after God had heard his side of the story, he would acquit him.

As the matter stood, however, God remained inaccessible to Job. No matter which direction Job turned, he could not find God (vv. 8-9). Verse 10 provides a glimmer of hope in all the gloom. Job had a temporary flash of recognition that his sufferings had been a testing process and that he would emerge purified like gold.

Job reaffirmed his position. He had not broken God's laws; in fact, he had treasured them. Regardless, Job knew that he could not change God's mind about his innocence. He feared that what had happened thus far had only been the beginning, not the end, of God's chastening.

When Job thought of God, he trembled and became fainthearted. Job felt "hemmed in" (v. 17) by darkness, possibly a reference to his sadness over God's apparent indifference to his pain.

General observations about injustices (24:1-25).—Chapter 24 resurfaces the puzzling problem of why the wicked prosper and the righteous do not. The speaker wondered why God did not bring judgment upon those who broke his laws. Included among the lawbreakers were flock rustlers (v. 2) and oppressors of orphans, widows, and other poor people (vv. 3-4).

Momentarily the speaker's attention turned to the plight of the victims of these crimes. These poverty-stricken persons have to scrounge for food like wild asses in the desert. They have no covering to protect them from the cold night air, nor shelter from the rain (vv. 5-8).

Verse 9 returns to the deplorable conduct of the wicked. They snatched fatherless children from their mothers' breasts. They even took the infants of poor people as a pledge for loans. (This action frequently involved enslavement of the child.) The kind of conduct described here ran completely contrary to God's law.

The predicament of the poor came again to the speaker's mind. Because of the greed of the wealthy, the unclothed field workers went hungry although there was food all around them. Olive trees (v. 11) symbolized wealth. The poor people pressed the oil that made the owners wealthy. They treaded the winepresses yet suffered from unquenched thirst.

The speaker maintained that not only the field workers but also the poor people who lived in the cities suffered as a result of wicked oppression. Dying people groaned and the wounded cried for help, yet God did not heed their prayer (v. 12). Murderers could not wait to murder the poor or to steal from them. Adulterers waited for the darkness eagerly so that they could perform their evil deeds. Unlike righteous people, they welcomed, rather than feared the darkness. Darkness was less hostile to these persons than daylight because it hid their evil deeds (v. 17).

The content of verses 1-17 could have come either from the mouth of Job or one of the friends. Laments about the injustice of the prosperity of evil persons were very common in Old Testament times. However, the next verses (vv. 18-25) contain thoughts contradictory to the arguments previously given by Job. For that reason many interpreters believe that chapter 24 came from the mouth of one of the friends. If the whole chapter did not come from one of Job's friends, at least verses 18-25 likely did.

Verses 18-25 deal with the fate of the wicked. The Revised Standard Version adds the words "You say" to verse 18 to indicate that Job was quoting from his friend's statements. However, the words "You say" do not appear in the original Hebrew. Most likely the whole chapter consists of a speech by one of the friends. In that case these added words become unnecessary.

The speaker used several figures to describe the fate of evil people. He said that the waters carry evil people away like scum or light trash (v. 18). In addition, because of their cursed fields they cannot get laborers (v. 18). Sheol snatches away these sinners in much the same way that drought and heat dry up snow waters (v. 19). Verse 21 returns briefly to the topic of the sins of evil people. In this verse the speaker tells how they oppress barren women and widows.

In verses 22-24 the speaker said, in essence, that God still rules the universe. He gives hope to the despairing and security to the unsupported, looking out for their welfare. He allows the wicked to prosper for awhile, but they will soon wither and fade like a flowering plant ("mallow") and be cut down like heads of grain.

The speaker concluded with a challenge. He dared his listeners to disprove what he had said, thus making him a liar (v. 25).

Bildad: Third Round (25:1-6)

Some interpreters call Bildad's brief speech in chapter 25 a doxology. It projects no new arguments, nor does it relate to the preceding speech. The speech merely points out God's majestic greatness in contrast to man's insignificance.

Bildad began the speech with a reference to the dominion and awe of God. The words "he makes peace in his high heaven" (v. 2) do not refer to peace in the sense of mere calmness or harmony. They allude to control and discipline. Bildad said that God controlled his numerous celestial armies. His light penetrated every place.

The point of Bildad's doxology appears in verses 4-6. How can a mere mortal being appear righteous in God's sight? God's penetrating light will surely detect a person's unworthiness. If God does not consider the moon bright or the stars clean, why would he deem human beings worthy? According to Bildad, mankind is only a maggot or worm (v. 6—symbol of extreme abasement).

Job's Response (26:1-4)

Verses 1-4 contain Job's brief but biting rebuke of his friends. Regardless of their original intentions, the friends had brought little consolation to Job. They had judged Job, rather than assisted and strengthened him (v. 2). They had acted as though they knew everything and he knew nothing (v. 3). Rarely does that type of counsel heal the sufferer.

In verse 4 Job raised a question that cast doubt on the validity of his friends' counsel. In essence he asked: Who is the source of your advice anyhow? Whose wisdom do you reflect? Job's implication stung more than his actual words. His question suggested the possibility that his friends had received their help from an evil spirit instead of from God.

Job's frustration and bitterness are quite understandable. His friends had misjudged him, rebuked him, and done little to minister to him. However, in fairness the reader needs to remember that the friends did travel a considerable distance in order to mourn with Job and that they cared enough to counsel him. They had no way of knowing that Job's suffering had resulted from a testing, not from sin. They likely viewed themselves as agents of redemption.

Bildad's Psalm (26:5-14)

Nestled between Job's satirical words in verses 1-4 and his insistence of innocence in 27:1-7 is a psalm about God's power. The psalm likely came from the lips of Bildad, since it so well fits the line of thought found in Bildad's speech in chapter 25. However, the writer did not positively identify the speaker.

The climax of the hymn (v. 14b) expresses the question in every worshiper's heart: Who can understand the power of God? God makes the underworld ("shades" and "waters") tremble. He uncovers the abode of the dead ("Sheol") and the place of destruction ("Abaddon"). He stretches out the heavens as one might stretch out tent coverings between poles and hangs the earth upon nothing (vv. 5-7).

The description of God's power continues in verses 8-14. God collects water and binds it into clouds (a reference to the cloud-rain process). He makes the horizon and the arc that divides day from night. The powerful "pillars of heaven" tremble at God's rebuke. "Rahab" (the chaotic power defeated by God at creation) stills at his command. God's spirit ("wind") makes the heavens fair; his power ("hand") destroys the "serpent" (symbol of evil).

The point of the psalm is that an omnipotent God controls the universe. If Bildad spoke these words, as most interpreters think, he likely did it to point out God's power and wisdom in contrast to Job's weakness and lack of understanding.

Job's Response (27:1-7)

The words "And Job again took up his discourse" (v. 1) help support the view that the psalm about God's power in 26:5-14 had not come from Job's lips. Otherwise the notation would be unneeded.

Verses 1-7 contain a reaffirmation of Job's innocence. "As God lives" (v. 2) was an oath of the most binding kind. Job defended his innocence to the uttermost. He swore by the God whom he believed had not carried out the due course of justice in his case. ("As God lives" were not curse words but rather words that assured the truth of the statements to follow.)

Job said that for as long as he lived, he would not lie. This assertion carries two thoughts: (1) Job would neither deceive them or God about his conduct, and (2) he would not confess guilt when he was innocent. He further asserted that to the very end he would hold fast to a claim of righteousness. He had a clear conscience.

Job concluded this discourse by expressing the hope that God would punish his enemies and find him innocent (v. 7). The statement contains both a curse on Job's enemies and a desire for blessing and vindication in God's courtroom.

Zophar: Third Round (27:8-23)

Again the narrative moves to a new speaker without identifying him. Interpreters generally agree, however, that the speaker in verses 8-23 was not Job. These verses deal with the fate of the wicked, a recurrent theme of Job's friends. Zophar seems the most likely speaker here since he speaks nowhere else in the third round.

The speaker inquired what hope "the godless" have when the crisis of death comes near. That question led him to ask whether God would hear a godless person's cry, or for that matter, whether a wicked person would even pray (v. 10).

The speaker proposed to teach his listeners exactly what the godless person can expect from God. His punishment will include the following disasters. If he has many children, they will either die from the sword or hunger (v. 14). He cannot use the silver and clothing he accumulates; it will end up in the possession of righteous persons instead (vv. 16-17). His house will collapse like a spider web (v. 18). He will go to bed wealthy and wake up poor (v. 19). Death will come to him in the form of a flood or whirlwind that will hurl him unmercifully and scorn him (vv. 20-23).

In brief, the wicked man activates his own hopeless fate through his continuous sin. The unrepentant sinner can expect no mercy.

Wisdom Poem (28:1-28)

The introduction to this commentary on Job referred to the book as "wisdom literature." Chapter 28 illustrates the wisdom element in the book to a high degree.

The writer does not name the speaker in this chapter. Some interpreters believe that the wisdom poem came from Job's mouth; others prefer Bildad, Zophar, or the person who recorded the "Yahweh speeches" (speeches of the Lord). However, the uncertain identity of the speaker does not detract from the message of the passage and its richness of imagery.

Chapter 28 (a wisdom poem) contains several important teachings. (1) Mankind has the ability to perform challenging deeds, including finding, extracting, and refining precious metals and gems. (2) Mankind's limitations, nevertheless, preclude the ability to find or buy the precious commodity known as wisdom. (3) God alone has absolute wisdom. True wisdom is a divine attribute not fully accessible to human beings.

Verses 1-11 illustrate what mankind can do. Throughout the ages man has made some remarkable progress. He has learned how to mine precious metals and gems and refine them. Sometimes he has had to travel long distances and expose himself to great perils in order to obtain these treasures (vv. 1-8).

Furthermore, man has shown his persistence and strength by

actually tunneling through rocky mountains to find his treasure. He has also penetrated watery depths in order to obtain it (vv. 9-11).

Man has proved that he can achieve outstanding feats. The writer did not minimize human ability. Nevertheless, the expected word "but" appears in verses 12-22. Humans have accomplished much, *but* they have their limitations. The next few verses focus on mankind's boundaries.

Verses 12-22 point to what people cannot do. Success was an integral part of wisdom. Wisdom, in its purest form, could not tolerate failure. Thus, if the wise man failed, he was not really wise. Job's friends probably viewed Job as one who had proved a lack of wisdom by his lack of current success. They attributed his loss of possessions and children, as well as his health failure, to a spiritual failure (sin).

Nevertheless, verses 12-22 relate to the general problem of finding true wisdom. They cite the fact that even the most successful person by secular standards finds pure wisdom inaccessible. Man seeks it everywhere but cannot find it (vv. 12-14). If he tries to buy it, he will find that it is not for sale; but even if it were, he could not afford to buy it (vv. 15-19).

These thoughts prompt the question of where wisdom abides. Obviously a person cannot find it, nor can keen-eyed birds see its hiding place. In fact, God put it to use when he successfully created nature. Wisdom enabled God to determine the force of the wind, measure out the waters, and decree the rainfall and the voice of thunder ("lightning of the thunder," v. 26). In summary, God acknowledged, appraised, established, and tested wisdom during the creative process. He knew how to put wisdom to the best possible use.

Since people could not discover for themselves how to find wisdom, God had to reveal it to them (v. 28). God said that the surest course to wisdom is to keep one's life free from sin. This advice refutes the idea that knowledge alone constitutes wisdom. Wisdom includes both a reverent relationship to God and obedience of his laws.

Job: Final Response in Third Round (29:1 to 31:40)

When people go through troubled times, they frequently wish for a return of the "good old days" when life ran more smoothly. Such was the case with Job. Chapter 29 contains Job's reminiscence of his past life when he experienced better days than his present ones.

Poem about the old times (29:2-25).—Job began his poetic reminiscence by recalling past times when God used to watch over him. God's favor ("light," v. 3*b*) had lit up his path. He remembered the friendship that he had enjoyed with God during his "autumn days" (harvest days in which he prospered). God had protected him at that time.

Job thought of the good life he had enjoyed then. His children still surrounded him. He used the figures of "steps . . . washed with milk" and "streams of oil" pouring from the rock (v. 6) to describe his life of plenty.

Another pleasant memory surfaced. He used to be the object of great respect when he went to the city gate, the center of judicial and business matters. Young men used to withdraw and older men rise to show their respect for Job. Even the ruling officers had quieted in his presence (vv. 9-10).

The reason for everybody's high respect for Job was his conduct. He had championed the cause of the poor, the fatherless, the dying, and the widow. He had clothed himself in righteousness and justice. Job had become eyes to the blind, feet to the lame, and an advocate to strangers. He "broke the fangs of the unrighteous,/and made him drop his prey from his teeth" (v. 17)—a figurative way of saying that he had rendered the unrighteous person helpless.

During those "good old days" Job had taken it for granted that because of his righteousness he would live to a ripe old age (v. 18). He had pictured himself as a tree planted in a well-watered area, healthy and vigorous. Some interpreters believe that Job referred to a palm tree here, since palm trees symbolized eternal youth. The last phrase of verse 20 ("my bow ever new in my hand") represented strength. Job thought his strength would always remain new—an implied contrast to the man with a broken bow (symbol of lack of power).

Verses 21-25 return to the thought of verses 2-17. In the past, men had really listened to Job when he spoke. In fact, they welcomed his counsel as a person would welcome the spring rain after a time of drought. Job showed his favor ("smiled," v. 24) on those who lacked confidence. They welcomed the light of Job's face. Job compared himself to a regal leader and compassionate pastor.

This chapter portrays life as it used to be for Job. It helps readers to recognize that Job had not always been a pitiful figure. He had known the sweet taste of success, a fact that his friends seemed to have overlooked.

Job's current suffering (30:1-31).—Chapters 29 and 30 might be called the "before and after" chapters. The former passage describes Job's joyous life *before* his trials began. The present one depicts the hard reality of his current suffering. In keeping with the blessing-curse theme throughout the book, chapter 29 represents Job's receipt of blessing and chapter 30, curse.

After years of living in the high esteem of his community, Job had suddenly become the object of ridicule. Young men, an age-group that traditionally honored their elders, laughed at him. In the past, Job would even have considered their fathers as being not as good as dogs (a figure of contempt based on ancient Semitic dislike of dogs). Job described these desert dwellers as scavengers, outcasts, senseless, and disreputable (vv. 3-8). Yet these were the people who now thought themselves better than Job, even to the point of spitting at him! (v. 10).

Job's enemies had interpreted Job's suffering to be a result of God's disfavor toward him. Therefore, they felt free to add to his suffering in any way they desired. Job said that they promoted his calamity, and no one restrained them (vv. 11-13).

Terror had beset Job's life. He had lost not only his dignity but also his total well-being (v. 15). Job felt drained of his vitality. He could not sleep at night because of the pain that bound him like a tight collar. He felt that God had "cast him in the mire" (an expression of instability, v. 19). He described this same instability in different imagery, that of dust and ashes that could blow away with the whim of the wind.

Job had experienced complete suffering: ridicule, bodily pain, and spiritual torment. He had already aired his complaints about his fellowmen and his physical distress. In verses 20-23 he made his complaint about the way *God* had treated him.

This sufferer felt that God had turned a deaf ear on his plea for help. The Hebrews considered alienation from God's fellowship the most devastating of all pain. Job viewed himself as an object that God had allowed his mighty wind to pick up and toss around. He felt sure that God intended to bring him to death (v. 23).

Job's existence had turned from music to mourning (vv. 24-31). He complained about the unfairness of his situation. Crying for help in a time of great need was a natural reaction—and for a righteous observer, so was a sympathetic response to the cry. Job had personally extended that kind of compassion to those who suffered. When Job himself cried for help, however, he not only did not receive a sympathetic response; he actually received even more trouble (v. 26). Job did not name God directly here as his oppressor, but he certainly implied it.

In verses 27-30, Job continued to describe his sufferings. He spoke of the inner turmoil that he constantly experienced. He said that he went about "blackened" (symbol of mourning—v. 28). He howled mournfully, like jackals howl at night in the desert and like the funereal sound of a crying ostrich (v. 29). Presumably verse 30 refers to the dread effects of his disease: his skin blackened and fell off, and his bones became feverish.

Previously Job had used his lyre and pipe (flute) to make music during religious festivals. Now they had become instruments of mourning in anticipation of his death (v. 31).

Final speech supporting Job's innocence (31:1-40).—Verses 3-15 contain Job's concluding defense relating to any sin that might have caused his suffering. In this speech Job systematically listed the sins commonly associated with divine punishment. He asserted his innocence in each instance. He used oaths to underscore his righteousness.

In studying this chapter the reader needs to compare Job's claims about his character with those recorded in chapter 1. God, too, had evaluated Job as "a blameless and upright man, who fears God and turns away from evil" (1:8). Actually the first verse in the book established Job's righteousness. Job, of course, still did not know what God had said. The following points were Job's defense.

1. Job had remained morally clean (vv. 1-4). Job stated that he had made a covenant to keep himself sexually pure. He believed that he would have been punished by God immediately otherwise.

2. Job had spoken only the truth and had lived in an honest manner (vv. 5-8). He swore that if he had lied, deceived, or acted in a dishonest way, he would not have been allowed to receive the fruit of his labor. The same punishment would have applied if he had stolen (reference to "cleaved to my hands," v. 7c).

3. Job had refused to be enticed (vv. 9-12). Job asserted that he had never committed adultery. He swore by the oath that if he did, he should be punished by having his wife taken as a slave at a mill. (Some interpreters note that "bow down" in v. 10 had sexual connotations. In that case the verse would mean that Job would have his wife given sexually to another man as punishment.)

4. Job had responded to the needs of his servants (vv. 3-15). He had never failed to heed his servants when they complained against him. He felt that he should look after his servants' welfare just as responsibly as God had looked after Job's own welfare in the past. The same Creator had made both servant and master.

5. Job had shown concern for the poor (vv. 16-23). Job said that he had ministered to the needs of poor people, widows, and orphans by offering food and clothes. He had provided the fleece of his own sheep to warm the loins of poor people and had pled the case of orphans at the center of justice ("gate"). Job said that if he had not done these things, his shoulder blade should fall from his shoulder and his arm be broken from its socket. He would have been terrorized by the thought of facing God's judgment if he had failed to help the helpless (v. 23).

6. Job had trusted in God, not in gold or in images (vv. 24-28). Job had not only refused to let gold become his god, but also had refrained from bragging about his wealth. Likewise, Job had not trusted in the sun or moon gods (v. 26). If he had, he would have deserved to receive punishment.

7. Job had shown no joy at the downfall of his enemies (vv. 29-30). He had rejected the practice of being glad when an enemy met destruction. He had not asked God to put a curse on the enemy.

8. Job had treated strangers kindly (vv. 31-34). He had offered hospitality to strangers and protected them from harm during their presence. (Hosts sometimes permitted, or personally engaged in, sexual abuse of strangers in their homes.)

Job swore that he had not been guilty of breaking any of this code of moral ethics. He had conducted himself in a righteous manner throughout his life.

For a long time Job had pled for God to listen to his side of the story, but he felt that God had not. He said that if only he had a document ("indictment") containing his plea, he would parade it in public so that all could see it. Job felt so self-confident about his innocence that he would have marched around boldly (vv. 35-37). Most interpreters believe that verses 38-40 belong elsewhere in the chapter. They contain another oath intended to affirm Job's innocence. This one relates to proper use of the land and fair treatment of its owners.

Chapter 31 concludes by stating that "the words of Job are ended." Job had consistently maintained his plea of innocence throughout the debate. Although Job had not convinced his friends, he never weakened in his conviction that he had not deserved this kind of severe punishment. Later passages show that Job's only real guilt came as a postscript to the onset of his suffering. In his zeal to defend himself he overstepped his bounds. People, no matter how righteous, cannot put themselves on an equal plane with the holy God in an argument. God alone has absolute wisdom in answering life's problems. To think otherwise is presumptuous.

The third round of the debate has brought up several truths that apply today. (1) God's transcendent nature does not prevent him from knowing what goes on in the lives of people. Persons must not assume that God is too far removed from humanity to care about their conduct or their suffering. (2) Sometimes God does seem inaccessible. Persons pray but think that God does not hear them. "Patient Job" showed his impatience at God's apparent hiddenness. However, in the future he would learn that God had heard him and cared about him after all. Many persons of today have made a similar discovery. (3) Confession and repentance are vital in order for a sinner to be in a right relationship with God. Their importance should not be minimized. Nevertheless, a confession of guilt where guilt does not exist is shallow. God does not require false confession and repentance, given only for the sake of expediency. He requires confession and repentance based on a recognition of guilt.

Elihu Prepares Ground for God's Speeches
32:1 to 37:24

Chapter 32 introduces another major division in the book. During the debate only Job, Eliphaz, Bildad, and Zophar spoke. The writer gave no hint of the presence of anyone else. Therefore, the appearance of Elihu's name in chapter 32 comes as a surprise.

Elihu's name means "he is my God," suggesting that he came from a religious background. He was a Buzite. Genesis 22:20-21 lists Buz as a descendant of Abraham's brother. The fact that Elihu claimed to be younger than the other men provokes an interesting thought. Elihu had remained quiet earlier in deference to his elders. Nevertheless, the narrative indicates that Elihu, not his elders, became an instrument to prepare the ground for the speech of the Lord that followed.

Elihu's Speeches Begin (32:1-22)

Verse 1 informs the reader that the other three men had finally stopped arguing with Job. They could see that Job had no intention of retracting his oaths of innocence. In the meanwhile, although Elihu had listened silently up to that point, he became incensed at both Job and the friends. Elihu was angry at Job for justifying his own actions instead of God's and at the friends for not pursuing the argument any further (vv. 2-5). Thus, chapter 32 begins with a speech of Elihu that deals with the Joban problem.

A new look at wisdom (32:6-22).—In biblical times people automatically assumed that old age and wisdom went hand in hand. They based this assumption on the premise that older people had more time to acquire knowledge and a wider range of experience. Elihu's initial silence illustrates this belief. However, his observation of Job and the friends had dispelled that view. He had come to see that old age had nothing to do with wisdom. Men acquired wisdom because God endowed them with it, not because they had reached a certain age plateau. Therefore, Elihu felt justified in declaring his opinion, even though he was younger than they (v. 10).

Elihu remained on the defensive, however, in spite of his radical view about age and wisdom. He reiterated how he had listened for their wise sayings, giving them his full attention. Not one of them had convinced Job of his error. Elihu warned his elders that if they thought they had shown wisdom, they were wrong. He maintained that all they had done was give up and thrust the matter in God's hands. Elihu indicated that he would not use the friends' arguments when *he* confronted Job (vv. 11-14).

In verse 5 Elihu had already revealed anger because of his elders' inability to refute Job. He underscored the same criticism in verse 15. He reasoned that there was no point in waiting any longer. Verses 18-20 indicate that Elihu was actually just "bursting" to speak. Unlike his elders, he would not soften the blow with flattery, lest his Maker "put an end" to him (v. 22).

God's Redemptive Purpose (33:1-33)

Having justified his reason for speaking, Elihu addressed Job directly. He challenged Job to listen, then to try to refute the charges. Elihu reminded Job that Job need not fear *him*, since he was merely another human like Job (v. 6)—an apparent allusion to Job's statement in 13:21 that *God's* hand terrified him.

At that point Elihu was ready to lay down the charges. He began by quoting Job's claim that God had punished him unjustly (vv. 8-11). Although Elihu voiced Job's basic complaint, he obviously misconstrued Job's plea of innocence. Job's point had been that he had not sinned seriously enough to deserve punishment of this magnitude, not that he had lived a totally sinless life.

Elihu confronted Job head-on. He asserted that Job had erred in thinking that man was as great as God (v. 12). This statement implied that Job thought himself greater than God, a claim never made by Job. Elihu then dealt with Job's complaint that God had not answered him. Elihu contended that mankind's failure to recognize God's answer did not mean God had not answered. He told Job that sometimes God gives his warnings in a dream. This statement likely came as no surprise to Job, who had already told of some terrifying dream experiences of his own. (See 7:13-14.)

According to Elihu, the dream warnings had two goals: (1) to cause repentance, and (2) to chasten. Both of them had a redemptive purpose. Verse 17 implies that if Job responded to God's dream warning by repenting, his days would be extended. The next few verses hint that God had chastened Job through pain to prepare him for restoration. In verse 23 Elihu probably meant that a divine mediator or some righteous person would serve as an intercessor for Job.

Elihu anticipated that when Job confessed and repented, he would regain his vigor and youthful appearance. At that time Job would recount to others how God delivered him from death ("the Pit," v. 30) and brought light to his life again. Elihu affirmed that

God works constantly ("twice, three times", v. 29) with man to redeem him from death and enlighten his existence.

Following these words, Elihu offered Job the opportunity to justify himself. Verse 33 says in effect: Unless you have a rebuttal, listen silently to me. I will teach you wisdom.

Defense of God's Justice (34:1 to 35:16)

Chapter 34 opens with a scene that resembles a home setting in which the parents discuss their child as though he were not there. Elihu spoke of Job in the third person, rather than addressing him personally. In the previous chapter Elihu had offered to teach Job wisdom; here he appears to be trying to teach it to the other three men also. This speech deals primarily with the righteousness of God's justice.

Elihu assumes leadership role (34:1-30).—Elihu had already expressed his discontent with his elders' ineffective counsel to Job (32:11-12). He said that at last he felt free to speak out. At this point the younger man assumed the leadership role of his elders in the Job dispute.

Young Elihu invited his elders to join in reviewing the case and deciding who was right (v. 4). He reminded them that Job had claimed innocence. Job had reasoned that the suffering God had brought on him had only made him appear guilty when he was not.

Having stated Job's claim, Elihu clarified his own stand. Some of Job's earlier statements had obviously disturbed him, but especially the one quoted in verse 9. Elihu said that only a scoffer would say what Job had said, namely that man gains nothing from delighting in God (an apparent reference to Job's words in 9:22).

Elihu's defense of God's justice begins in verse 10 and continues to the end of the next chapter. The basis of Elihu's defense lay in the fact that God and wickedness are incompatible. He believed that God consistently rewards and punishes according to a person's works (v. 12). Elihu reminded his listeners that human beings would not even be alive if God had not created the universe and everything in it.

Elihu's argument in verses 16-20 applied well to ideal standards for human leaders, but realistically not all officials meet these standards. Elihu's point was that God's righteousness far exceeded that of good earthly rulers. Wealthy rulers and poor people receive the same kind of justice from God.

Next Elihu pointed out God's omniscience (vv. 21-30). He spoke of how God sees every move a person makes; darkness cannot hide the deeds of an evil person. God knows the guilt or innocence of people without having to appoint a time to hear the case (a probable reference to Job's demand to have a hearing with God—9:32 and 14:13). Elihu asked what right a person had to condemn God for remaining silent. God does not need anyone to teach him justice.

Elihu confronts Job (34:31-37).—As indicated earlier, Elihu had directed the earlier part of this speech to Job's friends. In verses 31-37, however, Elihu confronted Job head-on. He asked Job if he had ever heard of a punished sinner who repented and recognized that he needed to be taught righteousness. Pressing further, he asked if God had to have Job's approval in making his decision about forgiveness. He egged Job on by saying: "Declare what you know" (v. 33).

Elihu knew how wise men would answer. They would say that Job did not know what he was talking about. If Job went on trial he would answer in the manner of a wicked person. Elihu agreed with the other wise men that Job had rebelled against God, mocking God by his clapping gesture.

Elihu's second speech (vv. 1-37) had left little doubt as to Elihu's stance regarding Job. Elihu agreed with his elders that Job's suffering had resulted from sin and that Job had compounded his sin by refusing to admit his guilt.

Elihu defends God (35:1-16).—At various times Job had implied or stated outright that his past righteousness had profited him nothing. He had felt that he had ample cause to complain. Elihu dealt with these statements in his third speech (ch. 35). His third and fourth speeches particularly laid the groundwork for the speeches of God to follow.

Elihu began this lofty speech about God's greatness by telling Job and his friends that he would answer their charge against God (v. 4). Verse 4 implies that although Elihu agreed with the friends on the issue of Job's suffering-sin relationship, he did not agree with all their conclusions. Thus, Elihu directed these words not only to Job but also to his friends.

Elihu summoned his listeners to consider God's supreme position. He said that God's heavenly status did not depend on what people did or did not do. The sinner, not God, bore the consequences of human sin, or conversely the reward of human righteousness (vv. 6-7).

Verses 9-11 describe a type of problem that still exists today. People forget to thank God when life runs smoothly, but when trouble comes, they suddenly become very demanding toward God. No wonder God refuses to listen to them (v. 12).

Elihu maintained that Job showed this kind of presumptive attitude when he charged God with hiding from him and impatiently demanded a hearing (23:9 and 24:1). Furthermore, according to Elihu, Job had accused God of not punishing the wicked. Elihu charged Job with not knowing as much as he thought he knew. He said that Job "multiplies words without knowledge" (v. 16).

Elihu's Concluding Statements (36:1 to 37:24)

The fourth speech of Elihu opens with the assertion that Elihu had something else to say on God's behalf (vv. 1-2). He assured his listeners that they could hear him with confidence because he spoke with full knowledge.

God's dependable justice (36:5-21).—Elihu had several points to establish that were basic to an understanding of Job's situation. Chapter 36, therefore, contains both a defense of God's justice and an application of it to Job's life. Elihu's main points included the following.

1. God does not act in an irresponsible manner. He neither rewards the wicked nor loses sight of the righteous (vv. 5-7).

2. God punishes for a redemptive purpose. He desires that sinners repent of their sins (vv. 8-10).

3. God shows his forgiveness of repentant sinners by restoring them to a prosperous and full life (v. 11).

4. God offers an opportunity to repent to all sinners, but if they refuse the opportunity they must bear the consequences (vv. 12-14).

5. God "delivers the afflicted by their affliction,/and opens their ear by adversity" (v. 15). Ideally, suffering becomes an instrument of learning that makes deliverance possible.

Most commentators agree that the meaning of verses 16-20 is uncertain. These words, a warning to Job, appear to refer to Job's former wealth. Elihu either charged Job with living in wealth but ignoring the needs of the poor, or in judging others harshly and himself too leniently. Elihu warned Job to *accept* his suffering ("ransom," v. 18*b*) instead of rebelling against God because of it. Elihu said that Job should resign himself to his plight and not be obsessed with the desire for death and divine judgment. Verse 21 suggests that Job's suffering may have come as a test. (See the translation of v. 21 in the NEB.)

"*We know him not*" *(36:22 to 37:13).*—Elihu's words in verse 26 ("we know him not") express the central thought in this passage. All his inspiring descriptions of God point back to the truth that the human mind cannot fathom God's greatness. Significantly, Elihu did not say "*Job* knows him not;" he said that "*we* know him not" (author's italics). Even the so-called "wise men" who claimed to know God had only a limited scope of knowledge. This was the common factor shared by Job, Eliphaz, Bildad, Zophar, and Elihu.

The body of this passage forms a hymn of praise to God for his unfathomable greatness. Elihu praised God for his power and wisdom (v. 22), righteousness (v. 23), and creativity and control of nature (36:27 to 37:12). Elihu summed up God's greatness in verse 13 when he said that whatever happens, God "causes it to happen." (Note: "Yahweh"—the name for God used by Hebrews—carries the meaning "He causes to happen.") Whether in winter storms, as in verses 1-13, or in the totality of existence, God makes things happen.

"*He is great in power and justice*" *(37:14-24).*—Elihu directly addressed Job before continuing his descriptions of God's greatness (v. 14). Verses 14-24 conclude Elihu's remarks in defense of God.

In verses 1-13 Elihu had poetically depicted the winter storms that God caused to happen. Verses 14-22 describe the summer storms.

Elihu referred first to God's command over the summer lightning and clouds. He reminded his listeners of how hot their garments felt during a sirocco ("south wind," v. 17) in the desert. He then used the figure of molten bronze mirrors to describe how the sky looked in the arid heat (v. 18). He spoke of the brightness of light when the wind passed (v. 21).

In verse 18 Elihu had asked if Job could duplicate what God had done. He pursued the thought in verse 23. Not only could humans not duplicate God's creations, they could not even "find" the Creator (a reference to God's transcendency). God's power, justice, and righteousness cause humans to stand in awe of him. The basis of true wisdom is fear of God, not self-conceit (v. 24).

Elihu obviously believed that Job's whole perspective of his suffering was wrong. In Elihu's view, Job should have submitted, not demanded; questioned his own motives, not God's; and acknowledged God's wisdom, not flaunted a self-acclaimed wisdom.

Speeches of the Lord
38:1 to 42:6

The introduction to the Job commentary explained the open-ended nature of the book. The writer posed questions, presented evidence, and let the reader arrive at a conclusion. Intermittently the characters probed the problems of faith and suffering in chapters 1—37. Job 38:1 to 42:6 contain the speeches of the Lord relating to the same topic. Here, as in the other speeches, however, many questions remain unanswered. On the one hand, this is part of the mystique of the book—every person finds that the final answer lies just beyond his reach. On the other hand, it is also part of the realism of the book. Life seldom holds any easy answers.

The Lord's First Speech (38:1 to 40:2)

The prologue to Job revealed that God knew Job's righteousness and trusted Job enough to let Satan test him. Nevertheless, God could not let some of Job's presumptuous demands during his suffering go unchallenged. The Lord's first speech focuses on them.

Where were you, Job? (38:1-11).—Although Elihu had misjudged Job, he had at least prepared the way for the speeches of the Lord to follow. The fact that the Lord appeared to Job in a whirlwind probably surprised Job less than that the "hidden" God appeared to him in any form.

The Lord began by accusing Job of doubting that God had a plan for the world (v. 2). God commanded Job to prepare like a warrior ("gird up your loins," v. 3) to defend himself against God's questions.

In 13:3 and 13:22, Job had demanded that God answer Job's questions; here, God demanded that Job answer God's questions.

Verses 4-11 deal with the wonders of creation. God outlined his laying of the foundation of the earth (vv. 4-7) and creation and control of the waters (vv. 8-11). In essence, the Lord asked: Where were you, Job, when I created the earth and sea? What makes you think that you know so much about my wisdom?

What have you done, Job? (38:12-38).—The Lord then turned to the matter of sustaining the universe. Again God bluntly reminded Job of how limited Job's wisdom really was. He asked what part Job had in operating nature's forces. Next, he asked Job if *he* had commanded dawn to shake out earth's skirts of darkness and to bring to light the creatures who had hidden there (vv. 12-13). God continued by asking if Job had ever entered the recesses of the sea or the gates of death (v. 17), or whether Job could even comprehend the expanse of the earth (v. 18). The Lord challenged Job to answer.

God pressed on with further questions. He asked: Did Job know where light and darkness dwelled so that he could lead them home? (vv. 19-20). God added that surely Job must know these matters since Job was so wise and old!

One by one the Lord named other forces of nature over which he had control—the storehouses of snow and hail that he used as weapons and the distribution of light and of the east wind (v. 24). God spoke of the floods that he had caused so that the dry desert would put forth grass upon which the lesser creatures could feed (vv. 25-27). He also reminded Job of God's creation of rain, dew, ice, and frost (vv. 28-30). Again, the implication was: What part did *you* play in these accomplishments?

Verses 31-38 focus on God's work in the heavens. Apparently the proper names listed here refer to star formations that rule the skies. God also mentioned the clouds, mist, and lightning that respond to God's call. (Some interpreters translate *mists* in v. 36 as "cock"—a bird noted for wisdom, including the ability to anticipate rain.) The point was that God, not Job, controlled the skies.

Can you control the animal world, Job? (38:39 to 39:30).—After pointing out his dominion over the heavens, the Lord focused on the animal world. Again the focus lay on what God could do, not what Job could do.

The Lord spoke of how he provided food for the young lions and baby ravens (38:39-41). God reminded Job of the divine wisdom relating to other parts of the animal world. He mentioned the gestation and birthing of wild mountain goats (ibex) and hinds (deer). He called attention to his control over the wild ass and wild ox (probably an Asiatic buffalo). Even the foolish ostrich received God's loving care (39:1-18). God asked if Job had given the mighty horse its strength, a power that enabled the horse to leap like a locust, paw violently, laugh at fear, carry weapons, race ("swallows the ground"), and wait eagerly for the trumpet call to battle.

God closed his account of the creation and dominion over the animal world with an observation about hawks and eagles. Pointedly, God asked Job if Job's wisdom had made the hawk soar or migrate. He inquired whether Job had caused the eagles to mount up and make nests in high places where they could spy out prey. Verse 30 relates to the proverb that eagles and vultures gather where there is a corpse. (Jesus referred to this proverb in Luke 17:37).

Conclusion to the Lord's first speech to Job (40:1-2).—The Lord had outlined his marvelous works in creating and operating the forces of nature, including animal life. His first speech had provided a panorama of wonders too great to comprehend. No one, including Job, could duplicate God's acts of wisdom and power. Knowing this fact full well, the Lord confronted Job with a challenge. He asked, in effect: Faultfinder, do you still wish to argue with the Almighty? If so, speak up (vv. 1-2).

Job's Response (40:3-5)

Throughout the debate with his friends, Job had correctly affirmed his basic innocence. However, the intensity of his suffering and his anguished search for a reason had caused Job to lose his objectivity. He had found fault with God for varied reasons: appearing to treat Job like an enemy, not being accessible, and seeming to act unjustly. Job had longed for an opportunity to confront God directly and plead his case.

That time had finally come, and when it came, Job had nothing to say. The accounts of God's greatness had suddenly made Job feel very small and insignificant. All that Job could do was lay his hand over his mouth to denote that God had silenced him. He had spoken before, but he would not do it again. The reality of facing God disturbed him more than he had anticipated.

The Lord's Second Speech (40:6 to 41:34)

God still had more to teach Job. The light had begun to dawn on Job, but Job had not fully come to terms with what had happened yet. The Lord's second speech, again from the whirlwind, supported and enlarged on his earlier points.

The divine challenge (40:7-14).—God had already challenged the "faultfinder" to respond once; here, he repeated the process. He commanded Job again to gird up his loins like a man (v. 7—an expression that described preparation for battle or quick flight). God had some more questions to ask Job. First, God asked if Job had condemned God in order to justify himself. Second, God inquired if Job had a strong arm and thunderous voice like God's (power symbols).

The Lord challenged Job to try carrying out the functions of God, such as abasing every haughty person and treading down every wicked one. Job had accused God of failing to fulfill the functions mentioned above. In verse 14 God told Job that if Job could successfully do what he criticized God for *not* doing, surely Job could save himself. The Lord implied that Job thought he could do a better job than his Creator.

The mighty Behemoth (40:15-24).—The word *Behemoth* (v. 15) may refer to a hippopotamus. This animal had the ability to destroy entire crops. His greatest strength was in his loins. (Strong loins denoted both bodily strength and sexual power.) Verses 20-24 illustrate how God provided for the needs of this large animal. He sustained him with food on the mountain, made a bed for him in the marshland, and shaded him with lotus trees and willows. God gave the animal courage to face the turbulence of the river without fear. Furthermore, he made the Behemoth hard to capture (v. 24).

The whole description of Behemoth points to the fact that human beings lacked the wisdom and creativity to make such an animal. Only God could create an animal like the powerful Behemoth.

The monster Leviathan (41:1-34).—Some interpreters believe that the Leviathan was a crocodile; others, a sea monster. This sea creature illustrated man's powerlessness to deal with God's mighty creatures. God said that even if man captured a Leviathan, he could never tame it (vv. 3-5). No trader would bargain for a Leviathan, and no man would lay hands on him more than once (v. 8).

Who could give Leviathan to God? It already belonged to him

(v. 11). These words may have been a veiled allusion to the fact that Job could not offer God anything, since God made all things; nor did God owe Job anything. (Previously, Job had demanded a hearing and vindication from God.)

Verses 13-34 describe the Leviathan's thick scales, fearsome teeth, strong back, and the flame-like spray that shot forth when he sneezed (vv. 13-21). These verses also describe the Leviathan's strong neck, pendulous folds of skin, stony heart, and ability to evoke fear when he raised himself (vv. 22-25). His underparts were like a piece of broken earthen vessel ("potsherd," v. 30). His presence caused the water in the sea to boil. He was a proud animal (v. 34).

The almighty God had used the examples of Behemoth and Leviathan as a stinging reminder to Job of the awesome power of the Lord. This was the same God whom Job, in his suffering, had challenged to answer him.

Job's Final Response (42:1-6)

By pointing out the magnitude of divine power, God had helped Job move from a self-centered view of God's purpose to a wider vision of God's design for the universe (v. 2). Job acknowledged that nothing could thwart the purposes of God. In verse 3 Job quoted a question from the Lord's earlier speech (38:2). Job had come to see that he had spoken without knowing what he was talking about— matters too wonderful for him to understand. Job had thought that he knew God fully in the past. Compared to his present knowledge, however, his past knowledge was like hearsay (v. 5). A firsthand experience with the Lord carries an impact that human instruction can never equal.

The interpretation of verse 6 requires careful thought. Why did Job say, "I despise myself,/and repent in dust and ashes"? Had Job concluded that his friends had been right and that his suffering had resulted from sin? Had he just come to understand more fully than ever before his own human limitations? Did he "repent" because he had failed to trust God to deliver him through his current suffering?

The author of Job provided no "pat answer." However, a review of Job's life shows that God viewed him as a "blameless and upright man, who fears God and turns away from evil" (1:8). Job had committed no sin grave enough to warrant the kind of suffering he had. Furthermore, God had shown enough confidence in Job to let

Satan test him under severe circumstances (1:12 and 2:6). Job's faith had proved strong through the loss of his livestock, servants, and his own children (1:13-22). Even when he received the affliction of sores from feet to head, he did not curse God (2:7-10).

Considering these facts, Job likely did not "repent" (v. 6) because he believed that his suffering had resulted from sin. Rather, he repented because he had not trusted God more completely and because his suffering prevented him from seeing God's omniscience in proper perspective. The epilogue supports these views.

Epilogue
42:7-17

The book ends on a positive note. Job received vindication for his innocent suffering and divine affirmation of his basic righteousness. Furthermore, the long view proved that the Lord was still a just God who acted with wisdom and integrity.

Nevertheless, the epilogue leaves unanswered questions. For example, why did God never let Job know that his suffering had resulted from a test designed by Satan? Why did Satan never receive a direct answer to the question, "Does Job fear God for nought?" (1:9)? Why do righteous people like Job often suffer while evil persons prosper? These and other unanswered questions lead again to the conclusion that the book deals more with faith than with the "Why?" of suffering.

Judgment on the Friends (42:7-9)

Verses 7-9 portray an ironic situation. The three friends who had judged Job so harshly became the target of judgment themselves. They had thought they had a corner on wisdom, but they actually had a shallow understanding of how God works. Job, too, had erred, but not so profoundly as the friends. Job had done right in defending his innocence and asserting that his pain had not resulted from sin.

The Lord directed his words of judgment toward Eliphaz, the eldest of the friends. God asserted that Eliphaz and his companions had misrepresented God (v. 7). Outwardly they had appeared to defend God, but they had really only defended their own narrow theology.

Verse 8 shows the seriousness of the sin committed by the friends. God promised that he would withhold the punishment they deserved only on the condition that they fulfill the following conditions. (1) They must take seven bulls and seven rams to Job to make a burnt offering—a number in excess of the amount usually required for individuals. (2) They must ask Job to intercede in their behalf. God would not let them pray for themselves since they had misrepresented God. The men did as God had instructed. They asked Job to pray for them, and the Lord honored Job's prayer (v. 9).

Job's Fortunes Restored (42:10-17)

God works in wise and wonderful ways. Although God had commended Job to the friends, he did not restore Job's fortunes until Job had actually interceded for them. Thus, Job had to pray for his friends' deliverance from God's wrath while he still had no hope for his own recovery. As an act of obedient faith, Job interceded for those who had wronged him.

Job was rewarded with restoration in four realms. He received twice as many possessions as he had before (vv. 10*b*,12). He was accepted socially again and received sympathy, comfort, and gifts from his relatives and friends (v. 11). He became the father of seven more sons and three more daughters to compensate for the ones taken from him (v. 13). He received the gift of longevity (vv. 16-17).

Surprisingly for that era, the narrative says more about Job's daughters than his sons. The narrator lists the names of the daughters: Jemimah ("dove"), Keziah (a cinnamon-scented perfume), and Kerenhappuch (a powder used for eye makeup). People regarded Job's daughters as the fairest of all women in the land. Furthermore, contrary to common practice, the daughters received an inheritance from their father that equaled their brothers'. (Daughters usually only received an inheritance if no sons existed.)

Another noteworthy comment appears in verses 16-17. Because of his severe affliction, Job had thought he was near death, yet verse 16 indicates that he lived 140 years longer. He lived long enough to see four generations.

The debate between Job and his friends concerning the mystery of suffering had begun with Job sitting among the ashes (2:8,13). The book concludes with God lifting Job from the ashes of life and restoring him to a joyous life-style. These scenes speak to readers of today who have felt God lifting them from their sorrow and restoring them to new hope.

Job also speaks to the current generation in other ways. Consider some of the insights from this ancient book.

1. For most persons, life consists of a series of ups and downs. The recurring theme of "blessing-curse" in Job is a realistic one. Sometimes life seems too good to be true; at other times the sorrow and pain seem unbearable. Earthly existence holds no guarantee of a trial-free life.

2. The problem of innocent suffering still looms in the world. Many righteous people face mental anguish, severe physical pain, and untimely death. Just as the pious platitudes of Job's "miserable comforters" (16:2) proved shallow, so the simplistic answers given by some well-meaning persons of today show little perception. Job never learned why he had to suffer innocently. Neither do some of the innocent sufferers of our generation.

3. Reward and restoration will eventually come to those who trust in the Lord. Job's restoration occurred on earth; some persons of today have also experienced miraculous relief from suffering on earth. For many innocent sufferers, however, the reward and restoration will come in life after death. Until then, life must remain a pilgrimage of faith for the righteous sufferer.